Be the Mira... Every Day !!

Unbreakable Spirit

Rising Above the Impossible

Linda J. Davis

Presented by

Lisa Nichols

Presented by: Lisa Nichols

Producer: Ruby Yeh

Editorial Director: AJ Harper

Print Management: Book Lab

Cover Design: Leo Herruzzo

Cover Poduction: Pearl Planet Design

Book Design & Typesetting: Chinook Design, Inc.

ISBN-13: 978–09819708-6-8

Printed in the United States of America

Yinspire Media
info@yinspiremedia.com
www.YinspireMedia.com

Contents

CONTENTS

CONTENTS

Lisa Nichols

Introduction

T he human spirit is unbreakable. That is not a notion up for debate; that is a *fact*.

Earlier this year I had the privilege of witnessing the truth of that statement, firsthand. I was asked to participate in the Table of Brotherhood, a national tour honoring the legacy of Dr. Martin Luther King Jr. The event was sponsored by General Motors and would culminate in the unveiling of the Dr. Martin Luther King Jr. Memorial in Washington, D.C.

I announced my role as Ambassador of Dynamic Dialog during a seminar I was teaching, and shortly thereafter I looked out into the audience and noticed a beautiful woman crying profusely. I had no idea what I was in for when I brought her up to the front of the room and asked, "Why are you crying?"

In her sixties, with long straight hair and porcelain skin, Shannon Peck stood before a room of forty people and began to tell a story that shifted the dynamics of the room. She took us back to Memphis, Tennessee in 1968.

"I was the manager of a hotel. Dr. King and his entourage walked in and asked to rent rooms, but I knew it was too dangerous for them to stay in the city, so I turned them away," she said, her eyes full of regret. "I told him, 'Dr. King, you *have* to leave Memphis *immediately*. The violence is getting out of hand.' I pleaded with him, but he insisted on staying to help continue his advocacy for the sanitation workers, who were on strike."

Shannon's shoulders began to shake at the memory of what came next. "Later that evening I was walking downtown with a date and I heard two gunshots. Pow! Pow! I knew instantly that Dr. King had been shot. My stomach dropped; the knot in my throat was so large I felt I couldn't breathe. I turned around and began to run, run, run, run, run."

With that Shannon began to cry, as though the tragic events of April 4, 1968 happened just yesterday. The whole room began to cry, full-on sobbing, for this is the part of the story where we all grieve. "As I ran, I couldn't shake the thought that Dr. King's dream of equality and civil rights would die with him," she continued. "I started shouting, 'How will the dream live? How will the dream live?' I felt so powerless."

What she said next stilled me. "Having you speak in honor of Dr. King's monument is just proof that his dream *will* live on. The dream will live on in people like you, and me—in all of us."

I watched Shannon's tears of sorrow—forty years' worth—turn to joy. And then all forty of the seminar participants encircled me. I felt hands from many countries, races and religions on me, and we stood in agreement. I cried so hard I could feel it in my belly, down to my soul. Every tear represented impossibility becoming possibility, separation joining in unity. And as I looked around at every face, I saw that Dr. King went to Memphis for this moment to occur. Dr. King marched on Washington for this moment to occur. We are all the benefactors of a dream fought for, died for, cried for and prayed for.

Dr. King's dream lives on in me, in you, in the authors in this book who shared their own true stories of experiencing the unbreakable, unshakable power of the human spirit. Let each page fortify you and give you hope; let each author's words envelop you in possibility as you, too, find the courage to get up and stay up, and fulfill the promise of your own dream.

Millicent St. Claire

Right Where I Needed to Be

J ail was no place for a woman like me—a mother, the wife of a respected doctor, one who simply acted in self-defense. During the three months I spent in county jail waiting to be transferred to prison, I did anything I could to get out of that dank, stinky, smoke-filled dorm. All around me women wailed against their pain and made one collect call after another, trying to get bond and looking for a way out of their self-created misery—and that included me. But for me, bond was not an option.

I attended every group meeting: bible study, church service; and although I didn't have any substance abuse issues, I even attended AA and NA meetings just to get out and get a breath of fresh air. At the close of one of the AA meetings, a facilitator said to all of us, "Just remember, your best thinking got you here." Bam! Her words hit me like a ton of bricks. I was crushed and stunned by the truth of those words.

Up until that moment I had convinced myself that I was the victim, even different than "those women," my fellow inmates. Yes, I shot and killed my second husband—but it was either him or me, and he'd been abusing me for way too long. In the end, I was convicted of voluntary manslaughter, but they were wrong. *So wrong. I don't deserve to be here.* Hearing the facilitator's words snapped me right out of my internal psychobabble, and I started to accept my reality.

I said to myself, *Whoa, my best thinking really does suck, because this is where it landed me.* That statement made me stop and take a hard, cold look at my life. I knew deep down inside that it wasn't one thing that led me here; it was a series of bad choices, and it was time to face the music.

Michael was a tall, charismatic and fascinating man who treated my two children and me with love and kindness—at first. He said, "Let me help you have the life you've always wanted to have. You don't have to struggle." He sold me a dream, and I bought

---

Your best thinking got you here.

---

the deal—but I didn't read the fine print. After a whirlwind three-month romance, I married a psychiatrist, but had no idea I had actually married a true-to-life Dr. Jekyll and Mr. Hyde.

Three months into the marriage Michael's dark side showed up. "Mr. Hyde" was a drug addict and sex fiend. At the end of his working day, he would get high, drink to excess, watch pornography and masturbate for hours on end. He wanted me to join him. I didn't mind some fun and a little puff now and then, but all of the excess was frightening and I remember saying to him, "Jesus Christ, Michael, a little fun is fun, but this isn't a way of life that I want to create and not what I signed up for. I'm a mother and a *person, not just an everyday sex toy.* I just want to be married and live a normal life. What's really going on?"

Whenever I resisted, things went from bad to worse and Michael got violent. The police came to our home many times on domestic violence calls. His drug abuse and bizarre sexual antics became overwhelming for me and I would realize again that the fantasy life of being married to a doctor was not all it was cracked up to be. I'd pack up my kids and leave. A few days later he'd call and beg me to come back with promises that things would change, and I would listen to his pleas, too caught up in the fantasy of the life he promised, of the love I so desperately wanted him to give. As a shrink, he knew my psycho-social history and he had my number.

The worst part was, nobody acknowledged my cries for help. Not the police or his colleagues, whom I begged to do an intervention. I was shunted aside and accused of being a hysteric. It wasn't until he had to be admitted into his own hospital that his colleagues took notice. He had overdosed at his drug dealer's house and on his way home, vomiting blood and convulsing. Now drastic measures had to be taken, because his medical community's reputation was at stake. While he was in the hospital, a tiny hope opened up inside me. *Maybe now that his colleagues see what's happening, we can get him some help and salvage this marriage.*

A day and a half after he was admitted to the hospital, Michael checked himself out and showed up back at the house. Wasn't he

---

*When I resisted, things went
from bad to worse.*

---

supposed to be getting treatment for his drug addiction? He hung out for a bit and then said, "I'm going out." I knew exactly where he was going—to Cody's house. Cody was his drug dealer.

Michael came back in the middle of the night and continued on his drug binge with liquor, porn, the whole nine. He ranted on about suicide and I'd usually plead with him not to talk like that, but the scene was all too familiar, right down to his ranting about Dr. Nicewander and his wife. Dr. Nicewander was a psychiatrist whose office Michael now occupied who, years before, killed his wife and then killed himself. This time, with a crazy look in his eye, Michael said, "We're going to end up just like them." *I don't think so,* I thought. But somehow I had a feeling that this was the night he would actually try to act on this insane notion.

He wanted me to have sex and get high with him, but I was turned off. When I refused, he became enraged. He kept coming into the room and leaving, like some revolving door, as he considered his next move. Covered in goosebumps, my whole body gripped with fear, I shouted, "Leave me alone! I just want out of this marriage!" He started choking me, shouting, "I'm going to kill you!" I struggled and managed to get away. I ran and got my gun. I didn't want to kill him, but I got the gun to keep him from killing me. In a rage, he stalked me through the house. He threw a drawer at me. I ducked, cowering near the bed. The drawer hit the bed and then I pointed the gun. It was the point of no return.

"Don't come at me! Don't you come at me!" I shouted.

He laughed and then roared, "What? A gun? Go ahead and shoot because I'm going to kill you, bitch." Shouting bizarre obscenities, he lunged at me and everything went into slow motion.

You're right where you need to be.

It was probably just a few seconds, but it felt like forever. I pulled the trigger and shot him, and then I watched as his body fell on the bed. Fearing he would fall on me, I jumped up. Then I just stood there in horror, looking at his body and caught in the impact of what had just happened.

With no self-defense laws in my state, I was up the creek. Despite the many police reports I had made for the many crimes committed against *me*, the relevant evidence I had was not included in the trial and the tables turned. *When did I become the bad guy?* I was sentenced to twelve years for voluntary manslaughter. I thought, *Our legal system is a total sham. I'm lucky I didn't get a life sentence.*

Your best thinking got you here. I kept hearing the facilitator's words replaying over and over in my head as I reviewed the events of my life. For months I stewed in jail, believing justice had not been served. But it was time for me to come out of denial and face the music. It was time to take total responsibility for my decisions that led up to that fateful night.

I bought into the dream he had offered me, of a comfortable life for me and my two kids and a happy marriage; and my need for safety and security and approval was so huge, I endured beatings, bruises, sexual humiliation, infidelity and pain. I wasn't a wife, I was a sex slave and a maid. Now I know that it wasn't just what happened in that marriage that went wrong for me; I had to accept all of the rotten choices that led me to prison. I arrived at a moment of complete and utter acceptance of my life when I realized: *It's not one thing that leads to a place like this, it's a whole string of events and a whole lot of stinking thinking.*

At that point I couldn't blame anyone for my life: not the District Attorney, not the judge, not the jury, not Michael's parents, not even him. It was all me. In a moment of clarity, I released the blame and accepted responsibility—and I felt as light as a feather. Telling the truth is strangely liberating, but no one said it would be pretty.

I looked around me at "those women," my fellow inmates, and I saw that their best thinking had gotten them here, too. I came to understand that they were wounded, just like me, vulnerable and in pain, and looking for a way out of their self-created misery, just like me. Although the names and faces change, we're all having the human experience and the crap is all essentially the same. I realized that I too was an addict, but of a different sort. I was addicted to negative thinking and drama. There was no denying it, as my life was a product of that negativity and its effects.

After three months in county jail, I was transported to prison. I remember being led to a group of raggedy old trailers surrounded by barbed wire—like an old army barracks or concentration camp. The guard pointed to my bed, one of fifty rusty bunks with gray wool blankets on it. She shouted some orders and then left. I walked over to an open window, looked out past the fence and wire and noticed a cow grazing in a beautiful, green glen. It was a perfect scene. Dumbstruck by the contrast between the beauty on the outside of the fence and the ugliness on the inside, I was moved simultaneously by the irony of the metaphor—I too was beautiful on the outside but ugly on the inside.

Then I felt a breeze caress me, and in that moment, something came over me. I felt as if God had taken me in his arms and held me. I heard a soft voice whisper in my ear, "I've got you, baby. You're right where you need to be." In that moment, I surrendered. I had made a mess of my life and it was true. In this ugly prison, I was in the perfect place to clean up my act and recreate myself.

I felt that God had put the brakes on me to help me realize that I had exercised my free will to create something other than life. I had created destruction. I asked myself, *If I created this, what else could I create? I have known the worst in myself, and now it's time for me to see the best. I can create destruction, or I can create something life-affirming and meaningful.*

For the next four years, until my release from prison, I worked in the law library Monday through Friday. This gave me time to read, pray, forgive and release my ridiculous past. With every thick, bound book I returned to the shelves, with every legal form I helped my cohorts fill out, I envisioned the life I would create and the change I would bring about in my community. As my fingers turned the pages of one law book after another, I was careful to take responsibility for every thought, word and deed. My new mantra was "self-correction, self-approval and, most important, self-love."

As strange as it was, I knew I was right where I needed to be. I was on that straight and narrow path to discover my true self and learn to create a life of joy and contribution in our world.

Millicent St. Claire is an AWE-THENTIC author, trainer and presenter. Clients learn faster and better in her sessions and have fun while learning to LIGMO! – Let It Go. Move On! She specializes in accelerated learning, neurolinguistic programming, hypnotherapy and other human development technologies. As founder of The LIGMO Institute, Inc., she travels extensively throughout the United States, offering one-of-a-kind, life-changing educational workshops and keynotes that get results. Sharing these programs is what she loves and is her personal "occu-passion." Millicent provides unforgettable presentations that will touch your heart, expand your mind and leave you wanting more! She is the author of the groundbreaking book, Simply Ridiculous. Connect with her at www. MillicentStClaire.com and www.LIGMO.com.

Kristina Paider

Cheesecake at Ground Zero

There it was: the remains of the World Trade Center. The sidewalk suddenly disappeared, swallowed up by the rubble. The stench from the burned metal and dust cloaked the air with a sobering, irrepressible grief. I marveled at New Yorkers as they bravely marched on, keeping the heart of the city beating. Now December, the focus was on recovery, searching for victims' remains.

New York was never really my thing. After the events of September 11, 2001, though, I felt called to be there. My international travels and experience as a journalist and PR rep, however, gave me no training for extreme disaster conditions, crime scenes or trauma relief. Still, this little voice inside me said "go."

I came on a sabbatical from work because I wanted be there. But deep down, I questioned whether I could handle it. Would I be so overcome with emotion, that the relief teams I was there to help would end up helping me? I thought about the nearly 3,000 victims and all of the people who loved them. My breath caught at the enormity of it all.

I climbed through an obstacle course of debris toward the Biodome, the huge, white, domed tent, nicknamed "the Taj," situated in the middle of the disaster site. It served as the central canteen and clean air space. Inside, it reminded me of the mess hall from *M*A*S*H*: simple and functional. There was a cafeteria line, dining area, and provisions. I remember sitting at my dad's feet as he watched re-runs of this show about the Korean War when I was little. But here, there were no doctors; only coroners.

I was briefed that the Salvation Army's effort, "Operation Compassion Under Fire," was as much about trauma support as it was about serving meals. My job was to connect with every person I could—to help them decompress and mitigate grief. "It's intense here," the Canteen Manager warned me, "and it's not for everyone." I braced myself. *Holy shit. This is for real.* I summoned all of my courage, and joined the serving side of the cafeteria line with the other volunteers. I watched the workers come toward me in their bulky firefighting uniforms and hard hats, shoulders slumped, eyes down. They shuffled through the line with an eerie silence. My impulse to say hello seemed out of place, so I stifled it. No one uttered a word. About one out of thirty made eye contact. They were physically and emotionally devastated. This is what Ground Zero looked like on the inside. Tears shot to my eyes and in that moment I could've cried a thousand rivers.

But a strong voice riled up inside me. *If you want to cry, cry with them, not at them.* In a sharp breath, I composed myself and turned back to scooping and serving veggies. In a quiet moment, I asked the woman next to me if this was normal. "Sometimes I ask them if they want more potatoes," she said. In between the rushes, I walked from table to table, searching for the grace to offer some meaningful words. There were none to be found.

Days passed and many of the firefighters remained in shut-down mode. Knowing the power of even a moment of relief, I wanted so desperately to find them one—to find anything to break up the anguish. Instead, it felt as if grief was prevailing. I was stuck, not knowing what to say or do. The same inner voice that urged me to just "go" now said, *You know, better than maybe anyone here, what to say.* No I don't. *Yes. You do.* Half-wondering whether I was developing a split personality, my thoughts wandered back to my own personal ground zero....

It was Easter. I had opened the door to a huge, three-foot stuffed bunny and a basket that spilled over with an insane amount of candy. Behind this was my boyfriend, who entered the scene pouring out soap-opera proclamations of love and devotion. As we talked, he realized that I had smoked. I had no idea he hated smoke so much until that very moment when, like the flip of a switch, everything changed.

I blacked out, briefly, then came to, lying on top of a now broken space heater, the wind knocked out of me. Instinctively, I touched my head. There was no blood, just intense throbbing. He had shoved me, and as I fought for air, I realized I never saw him so possessed by his rage. I ran down the hall, shouting for my life. I

Like the flip of a switch, everything changed.

---

threw open the first door, and squeezed between a chair and the wall. I continued yelling for help, pleading with him, and making one hundred deals with God as he lunged at me, continuing his tirade of violence and atrocities. Thankfully, my aunt and uncle came in and pulled him off.

I was seventeen when I met him, a sociopath disguised as a charming boyfriend. In the four years we were together, I was threatened, choked, betrayed, body-slammed and terrorized. I ran on glass, lost my vision and put my family, friends and roommates in danger before I moved out of the country and ended it. I felt shame. *How could I have let this terrorist in our front door? What kind of example am I for my sister?* She was thirteen years old. I knew I had to do better.

But before I could do anything, I sank into a toxic cocktail of sadness, despair and grief.

What followed was isolation—the worst part. Worse than the physical pain, worse than the confusion and the mind games, was the feeling that I was alone. The reality was unimaginable, even to me, and I was living it. It was like being awake in some weird nightmare. I shut down and pushed people out—the same way the

11

firefighters were doing now. And the isolation hurt like a thousand razor blades.

By the time I was twenty, I was on my fifth life, and I knew that the timing, interventions and luck that graced my life had to be more than coincidence. There was a bigger plan for me. I tried to think about what would've helped me then. What I wanted was someone who understood me without my having to explain a word. Someone who could stand by my side, in all of the ugliness of this mess, and keep me company while I walked through it. Ten countries and several months later, I found myself disco dancing in a friend's living room at two in the morning, totally lost in the moment. It was a small moment, but a big turning point. I had found my smile again.

Back at Ground Zero, as I walked through the dining area, I noticed a burly man sitting alone. By this time, even though I had calibrated to the norm of the situation, I could see that this linebacker-sized guy, who would probably give you the shirt off his

---

The reality was unimaginable.

---

back and walk into fire any day of the week, was not all right. I sat down next to him, not saying a word. I knew there weren't any. I stayed by his side for a long time. It was a bit awkward, I have to admit; not saying anything, not looking at each other. He was in anguish. *Stay with it*, directed my inner voice.

I sensed, or maybe even projected, an internal wrestling. A trying-to-make-sense of the completely senseless. I watched his face, reflecting gut-wrenching emotion. I wondered if he had found remains, if he *hadn't* found remains, if he had lost his colleague or a brother, or more. I wondered if he felt alone, even in this room full of people. He still had not looked at me. I gently put my hand on his forearm, and gathered up my courage, emotion choking my words, tears on standby. As boldly as I could I said, "Let it out." It came out as a whisper. But he heard me. He lifted his gaze ever so slightly. And he put his head in his hands and wept. "It's okay,"

I reassured, scared and calm at once. "Just let it out," I repeated, stronger. I had so much more to say, but no words for any of it. I could no longer hold in the sadness or the tears, and I cried along with him. With that, something shifted.

Not long afterward, I was assigned to run the dessert station. It kind of felt like a mini-promotion in volunteer-land, and I welcomed the change. The canteen manager told me dessert was significant. I, of course, knew that. It was the time of day when

You are gentlemen in the truest sense of the word.

the relief workers were most likely to relax and connect and this break was the most critical to their well-being. Indeed, there was a distinct difference in the relief workers when they came through this line. They tended to eat dinner first, then come back for dessert, visibly more relaxed. We had eye contact.

One night, I had Eli's Cheesecake on deck. To this crew it was the holy grail of dessert. I even saw their eyes twinkle as slices of cheesecake flew off my little countertop. And before I knew it, I was on the last piece. But—unbelievably—no one would take it! The NYFD apparently has a code for cheesecake. Firefighter after firefighter came by, eyes lighting up, the one happy thought they may have had all day, and every one of them declined.

"It's the last piece? I'll leave it for the next guy," they'd say. *What?!! Are you kidding me?* My inner voice and I finally aligned. Their brotherhood was humbling, but I had to put my foot down.

Dear firefighters, I mused to myself, *you are doing the hardest job on earth. You are gentlemen in the truest sense of the word. I respect you immensely. I wish the rest of the world would model your code of conduct. But dessert is where I draw the line. I am going to make my own code, I'm going to call it "slivers." And I'm gonna to ask you to follow it.*

I cut the last piece of cheesecake into ten little slivers. Instead of letting the firemen breeze on by, I stopped them, making them wait until there was a group of ten. We all counted together... "One… two…three"—and they took their slivers at exactly the same time. That way, no one would have the last piece. Did they look at me oddly? For sure. Did they think I was a little crazy? You bet. But did they love it? Yes.

It was getting closer to Christmas. The rescue workers put a tree up in the middle of the disaster area, ran lights and lit it: another sign of their spirit and resilience that inspired our nation. We received more and more cheesecake, and sometimes we'd do my ritual multiple times per night.

My dessert code encouraged meandering and small talk, if nothing else, about why I was making them stand there. It was a start. I told them that I represented tens of thousands of people who would be there to help if they could. I thanked them for what they were doing. These guys stood there, and thanked me back.

"Do you live in New York?" they'd ask.

"No. Chicago," I'd reply.

"You're on vacation?"

"No. I'm here just for this. I came here for you," I'd answer.

"Really? Why?" they'd ask.

"I had to," I'd say, looking at them squarely. When it got too intense, I'd look away and shrug. "Seems like you needed some help with this cheesecake thing." Just then, these weary, salt-of-the-earth, courageous, role models would do the most amazing thing. They'd crack a smile.

I knew that smile. It was a small sign, but it was enough.

Kristina Paider is a Hollywood screenwriter, award-winning marketing executive and global media consultant. Over the course of her career, she has worked with business leaders and media in thirty-four countries and in seven languages. Connect with her at www.KristinaPaider.com.

Allyson Byrd

Marvelously Made

In the darkened room, Laverne and Shirley dance across the TV screen as I wait for the fourth pizza delivery of the day. At eighteen, I've lost all my hope. I dropped out of high school at fifteen. I weigh well over three hundred pounds. I'm broke. I sleep around but never find love, and my friends are pimps, drug dealers and prostitutes. My family is completely exhausted by my continual bad choices. But this is me. This is my story.

With the strategic thinking I inherited from my father, I weigh my next move. I need money. My checks to the pizza place will bounce—all of them. *Which girls I know could I pimp out? I could run that crack house better—well, to start with, get a better product. Could I mobilize the drug dealers I've dated into an effective team? Or should I rob a bank.* In the end, my next move that makes the most sense is suicide. I can see no other way out.

By all odds, I should never have been born, and I know it. My mother had severe anemia, and after my sister was born breech, her skin blue, her blood like red water, the doctors advised Mom not to have another baby. Years later, she met Marcus, an Atlanta businessman who became the love of her life.

They married, and despite the doctors' warnings, she worked hard to become pregnant, and then used every method and home remedy she could find—eating tons of sweet potatoes, and drinking hot jello—to ensure I was healthy and eliminate the need for a blood transfusion when I was born.

But my father carried a deep, dark secret. He had killed a man in Chicago, and was living under a false identity. He quickly became controlling, abusive and violent. Just three months after I was born, she fled with us to her mother's house in Texas as soon as the outward signs of her still aching broken nose and cracked ribs disappeared. He wooed her back, but the beatings continued until he broke her love. Then my father's best friend called, telling her Marcus was really Eugene, a fugitive, and the FBI had found him and arrested him for murder.

Mom divorced Eugene and the last time I saw him was in prison when I was four. Years later his charge was reduced to manslaughter, and after an additional year he received release based on time served. Mom never made me think of my father as a bad man, and she always told me how much he loved me. But no one else in my

---

By all odds, I should never have
been born, and I know it.

---

family had been given this name—not my mother, not my father, not my sister. Allyson means nobility of truth, but I was born in a confluence of lies. Byrd was my father's alias, his flight name. He branded me with his crime, his bloodshed, his escape.

Mom raised us on food stamps, moving from place to place. In one of our residences, sometimes rats crawled across our feet as we slept. Once a new landlord had an easy solution to the blood still smeared on the walls: "We'll just paint over that."

But Eugene's absence was my greatest teacher. I had flight in my name and my DNA. There I was, living his path without his presence, without his voice. And though I lived in full-on, constant escape mode, I was always immobilized by my circumstances, always wondering, *Why, oh why, was I ever born?*

At age twelve, everything turned. My grandmother Octavia, my mother's mother, passed away. I spoke to my father for the very last time that year, and the loss of my loving grandmother and the only father I ever knew was too much. I began using escapism in earnest to disconnect from my feelings. I remember thinking, *I don't know who to be.* So I tried to become someone else.

One day I bought a new outfit from Wieners with $24 I saved up from babysitting. I looked in the mirror and didn't recognize myself. I was a little girl, trying to look so grown up. Again I thought, Who am I supposed to be in this moment? That night I went to a party, pretending to be someone other than me, and by the end of the night I had had sex with every man in the house. I moved from room to room on autopilot, letting men old enough to

---

But no one else in my family had been given this name—not my mother, not my father, not my sister.

---

know better direct me, take me, use me. It was as if the touching, the pressing down and the pushing in were happening to someone else. My body remained, but I had flown away.

When I was thirteen, my cousin Carmen told me, "I want you to remember Psalm 139. 'Oh yes, you shaped me first inside, then out; you formed me in my mother's womb.' That means God knew you before you were born. He sees your entire life from start to finish, and it is breathtaking. 'Body and soul, YOU are marvelously made.' *You*, Allyson." I read the entire passage over and over again. *How could He have known me and known this is what I would become? Why would He still say yes to that?*

Now, as I sit in the dark, contemplating the ultimate flight into the last darkness, I remember Carmen's lesson and think, *Ah, God, how could you know what I would become and still want me?* I can see no way to become something different in this life, no escape from my pain but flight.

Just as I'm starting to think seriously about a plan to end my life, the phone rings. It's Carmen, the only family member who still has hope for me. I feel a little of the darkness lifting the moment I hear her voice. She and her husband Tim were moving to Oklahoma. Would I stay with her while he went on ahead to pick out a house?

"Yeah," I say, gratefully. "That would be cool." I don't have to decide yet whether to stay or fly away. Even if I end up disappointing her, I can postpone my next move for a while. I spend seven days with her: no pizza, no darkness. Instead there is laughter. Fun. A sense of purpose and reconnection to life. But even with all of this, I still don't tell Carmen my secrets. I don't tell her that I have been contemplating suicide, that I've been stealing and hanging out in drug houses, that I have been letting my father's past define me. And because I've been keeping these things from her, no matter how much I want to, I can't stay.

I could feel the weight of my
father's legacy leave my body.

So I return home with my secrets, and immediately go back into the darkness. I walk back into my bedroom, turn out all the lights, pull out my checkbook and order pizza with money I don't have. My life is in as much debt as my checking account. The voice inside me that told me to play small has become my greatest influence.

Carmen calls me one night as I sat alone in the dark. "What are you doing?" she says. I hear the concern in her voice.

"Oh, you know. I just ordered a pizza."

She says, "I want you to cancel that order. Pack. We want you. Come move with us to Oklahoma. Allyson, you will live and not die. You will live a *life*, not just exist."

"We want you." Who ever wanted me? This was major. I packed my few clothes so fast.

Everyone told Carmen she was crazy to take me in, but the move was the jolt I needed. The change in zip code was my fresh start. That decision to move made all the difference in real movement in my life. And God became real to me. He became less of a dictator, more of a father and a creator.

At my first transformational workshop held by the Association for Christian Character Development, we were given an exercise. We were to tell the most tragic story of our lives. Easy: *My murderer dad abandoned me. I only exist because of his lies.* But then, according to the rules, I had to turn it around and tell the story from his point of view, tell how it all felt to him. And then I had to tell it as if I were Pollyanna, as if it was the best thing that ever happened. In that circle, I confronted every limiting belief I held. I confronted my story and it lost its power. It didn't hold me hostage anymore.

I could feel weight of my father's legacy leave my body. *You've always dreamed of flying,* I told myself. *Now you can use your wings—they haven't been clipped or tied down. You're free. Nothing is holding you back.* And just like that I could see the runway to my future, to all that was open to me. At last, I could stop pushing against the wind; at last I could soar. It was what I call a six-ounce healing. As I continued in transformational work, my capacity for healing and vision expanded. The deeper I would go in what was broken, the further I could soar in what was healed.

During my first, long phase of healing, I released 165 pounds. Then I got caught up in a story that wasn't my own and reabsorbed 85 pounds of it. I know now that I have a tendency to store other people's stuff and negativity in my arms and my thighs instead of processing and digesting it. I am always learning more about how *not* to take on others' stories and legacies.

Joseph Campbell said, "What all myths have to deal with is transformations of consciousness. You have been thinking one way, you now have to think a different way. Consciousness is transformed either by the trials themselves or by illuminating revelations. Trials and revelations are what it's all about."

People often ask, "What was the turning point for your life?" It was my transformation of consciousness and my willingness to accept God's final decision for my life; only then could I truly accept my mission to change the world. The means by which we come to that clarity is like the grit in the oyster that finally makes the pearl. When we stop thinking about the grit and focus on the pearl, we don't whine, "Oh, why am *I* here?" We don't wonder why we were born, or even think about suicide. The intonation changes and we ask, "Oh, why *am* I here?" It's the greatest question of humanity.

Everyone has a soul story we identify as our history, the unfolding of our present and the revelation of our future. It is the story God writes for us before we're born, before we're given names. It is not my story, or the name my dad handed down to me, or the story others tell me about myself. Our story, our *purpose*, exists in us regardless of our acknowledgment of it. *Body and soul, we are marvelously made.*

Allyson Byrd is a noted speaker, author and life coach who inspires people to live in purpose, embrace passion and achieve personal greatness. She teaches businesses and organizations how to remove obstacles from their culture, processes and people. In 2008, Allyson founded The Purpose Within as a unique tool to assist the average person's transition from "purpose discovery" to "purpose mastery."

Named San Antonio's Woman of Influence in 2010, cited in Who's Who in San Antonio and nominated for the National Association of Women Business Owners 2010-2011 Entrepreneurial Spirit Award, Allyson is the featured life coach on News 4 WOAI-TV's San Antonio Living and host of Love Yourself to Life! with Allyson Byrd on AM-630 KSLR Radio in South Texas. She has written two books: Love Yourself to Life: Breaking Limiting Beliefs on Love and When God Takes A Bath: Lessons of a Life Transformed. Contact Allyson at www.ThePurposeWithin.com.

Michelle Larson

The Only One

My father brought a gun into the house when I was an infant and slept with it under his pillow every night. He wasn't a hunter or a policeman; he was simply convinced that someone (everyone) was out to get us and he was going to blow their brains out if they tried.

Something would wake him and through the house he would dart, naked, gun in hand. He would hide behind doors, trying to be quiet, and then sometimes he would chase the phantom outside and down the street. I remember how frightened I was, lying in my pink-ruffled canopy bed, waiting for my father to find whomever was after us, coming for us, trying to hurt us... or worse.

Dad didn't just have the one gun; in addition to the one under the pillow, he had one under the bed, one in the closet, several in the garage and in his truck. For years, he even wore one in a holster around his calf. A collection of weaponry surrounded us: huge serrated knives, swords, rifles, handguns, pistols. I believe he felt that all of this was necessary to protect us. He took this role of "family protector" very seriously, and felt it was his job to keep us safe from all of those people out there who were plotting against us.

My father would tell me, "You will find out. I am the ONLY ONE." He told me he was the ONLY one I could really trust. The

ONLY one who would protect me from the scary world, full of danger. The ONLY one who would lay down his life for me.

My mother, on the other hand, would tell me, "Dream big. Go for it, girl. You can do anything you set your mind to." I became a product of both of their influences: independent, smart and ambitious, with a hidden fear that something bad was always around the corner. My grades were always good, my homework and chores done before asking. I never got into trouble, and did what I was told (mostly).

By age twenty-three, I was married and had started my own business. Within a few years I had two wonderful little boys and a career as an artist that I loved. The marriage didn't work out, and I divorced after twelve years. Though it was a difficult time, it also gave me the opportunity to grow as an individual in a way that was impossible before. So, off I went. My business skyrocketed, I

*He told me he was the ONLY
one I could really trust.*

bought property at the beach, traveled the globe with my children and expanded my creative horizons with travel writing and photography. But in the deepest part of me, I feared it was too good to be true. For all that I had accomplished, I couldn't shake the feeling that at a moment's notice it could all be taken away.

Then the bottom fell out. "I'm leaving your father," my mother said to me on the phone. I was surprised at her timing, since she had tolerated an unhappy marriage for forty-two years—I had just figured she was in it for the long haul. I was supportive, and we spoke for about an hour about the whens and hows, the details and worries. "I'm scared," she said. *I'm scared for you*, I thought. We both knew that Dad would *not* take the news well.

In the months it took for my mom to finally get the courage to leave, we had many phone conversations about her plans and our concerns. On the day she left, I called my dad to tell him that I was there for him. My breath caught in my throat when he said,

"I heard all of the conversations you had with your mother. You sided with her and I am never speaking to you again." (He had tapped the phone line.) Devastated, I cried and cried, sobbing uncontrollably for days. *How could I live a life without my father? I'm his little girl. He's the ONLY one who can protect me. If he's the ONLY one, what will happen to me?*

I waited a few months, and then I sent my father a letter pleading with him to reconsider his decision to eliminate me from his life. It took me two days to carefully choose my words. I knew that he would be triggered easily, so I read it to couple of people to make sure it projected just the right message for a positive response. The day after he got the letter, he called me. My heart raced when I answered my phone.

In a cold monotone, he said, "I got your letter. You think your mom is so innocent. I have evidence that she has been planning to steal my identity, take my family, and assets have been hidden. She wants to take everything that I have worked for my whole life. I know you probably don't believe this, but she has even planned on getting rid of me. She has a hit out on me. I haven't slept in a bed in three months, because I fear for my life. I have documentation to prove criminal activity. Eight to ten people's lives are going to be devastated by this whole thing. Heads will roll. When this shit hits, it will be all over the media. You are going to be blown away."

Stunned and baffled, I asked, "Dad, who are the eight to ten people? Is Mom one of those people? Am I one of them?"

He responded disdainfully, "You know who they are."

After a short silence, I asked, "Did you even read my letter?"

"Yeah," he said. "It's mostly bullshit."

That was the one and only actual conversation I had with my father in over four years. Knowing that he was in possession of an arsenal, wasn't sleeping, was having delusional thoughts and threatening lives, I wasn't sure what to do. I was afraid for my life, Mom's life and for anyone else who, in his mind, had wronged him and was on his list of "heads that were going to roll." *Everything is out of control. Am I in danger? Oh, God, what should I do?*

The man who was supposed to love me began to loathe me. After being subpoenaed, accused of hiding money for my mother and required to supply seven years of personal and business financial records, I sat in a deposition room with my father and his attorney. I was grilled with questions for hours while I sobbed, gasped and shook uncontrollably. My father glared at me from across the table like I was nobody. I felt his eyes on me, but I couldn't look at him.

I kept expecting him to break, come over to me, hug me and say, "Stop the questioning. I can't bear to see her like this." But he

----

I felt his eyes on me, but I couldn't look at him.

----

never did. The giant lump in my throat felt like a stabbing rock with sharp edges. *This is the ultimate betrayal.*

During this same period, the economy crashed. With it, my company's sales plummeted. The property at the beach was now worth far less than I'd paid for it. My 401K spiraled, like everyone else's, and with it my dreams of early retirement. All of this dropped me to my knees. I wanted to know: What was I meant to learn? What was the lesson in the pain? For two years I muddled through, silently crying myself to sleep, feeling hopeless. I tried so hard to pretend I was okay for everyone around me, but I was barely hanging on by my fingernails.

Then, like a miracle from cyberspace, I received an email inviting me to cover a spiritual retreat as a writer for an online travel magazine. I had never been one to sit in a pew on Sunday mornings, and I didn't really even know what "spiritual" meant, but I needed something, anything, to help pull me from the abyss I was spiraling into.

Twenty participants gathered in a dance studio on the fourth floor of a downtown high-rise in Manhattan. The first half of the day was spent in a circle, reviewing the Toltec philosophy and how we can apply it to our lives. "With awareness, we can take responsibility for our thoughts and actions. If we don't like where our lives are going, we should let go of old knowledge and bring in new knowledge. Reprogram and change our story. Instead of creating a novel too heavy to lift, filled with drama and tales of how we have been victimized, we can write a beautiful story that everyone wants to have a chapter in. We can make our lives something that we are happy to show up for."

Nervously, I raised my hand, "What if your story isn't something that is easily changed? What if your father has disowned you and your whole family is suffering because of it?" With heart racing and palms sweating, I agreed to be the protagonist in a pyschodrama. I was asked to choose someone from the group to stand in as my father, so that I could say everything I needed to say to him.

Swallowing deeply, and through gasps from crying, I said, "How could you disown me? What is wrong with you? Don't you have a heart? I have children and I can't imagine my life without them! You hold on to your anger like an appendage. How can you

---

*I resigned the idea of being able
to control anyone but me.*

---

be so cold?" I then switched roles and had to stand in my father's place. I responded as him speaking to me, "You just don't get it. I'm done with you people." This went on, back and forth, for about forty-five minutes. It was gut-wrenching, but I got through it. In the end, I felt sympathy for my father and I sent him love, knowing that I could have a happy life with or without him. I resigned the idea of being able to control anyone but me.

This experience became my awakening. It was the point where my life transformed from expecting that other people and my environment should make me happy, to taking responsibility for my own mental and emotional well-being. Truly miraculous!

Two days later, I walked through the city with twenty of my newest and closest friends. We were asked to keep our minds clear and focused on the answer, whatever that meant to each of us; and to look for something that was symbolic of our answer as we walked. I walked alone and took in the beauty of the fall leaves that covered the streets and sidewalks with a blanket of gold, amber and ruby. Reaching down, I picked up a perfect, bright, newly fallen leaf and decided that this was my answer.

A leaf holds tight to the tree until it can no longer hold on. Eventually it has no choice but to let go. The cool breeze picks it up and carries it away from the only place it has ever known, but the leaf knows it is time to fly and land where it may. I placed the leaf in my pocket. After a bit, I stopped in front of a beautiful group of tombstones outside a glorious old church and said goodbye to my old life, with gratitude for all that it had taught me. I released the leaf, watching it fall… letting go, letting go, letting go.

I hold no resentment or anger toward my father. I truly believe that all of it had to happen just as it did. He is on his own journey, and I will always love him and hope that someday he can release the heaviness that he carries in his heart. I believe that he loves me, but I have been able to let go of the little girl who is nothing without her father's love. All grown up, I have a new view of myself and what is possible. I am excited for the journey ahead. And I know now the ONLY person who must be there for me is ME.

Michelle Larson travels the world seeking enlightenment from a tapestry of inspiring shamans, priestesses, mystics, teachers and other extraordinary characters who have shared their path to peace. She founded Bliss Sisters, a women's group where she shares her magic toolbox for living a life free from fear, shame, regrets, expectations, judgment and limitations, and leads the ladies in meditation, manifestation and meaningful connection to themselves and each other. Michelle is the author of the forthcoming book, Bliss Bound—My Journey to Perfect Happiness. *Follow her Daily Bliss Tips on Facebook and read her blog, filled with stories of her wanderings, at www.Bliss-Sisters.com.*

Julia Taylor

Heartstrings

It was four days before Christmas when I called to make sure someone at the adoption agency would be there to sign for our dossier (our enormous collection of required, signed, and sealed original documents). Completing our paperwork was one of the final steps in our four-year journey to adopt a child—we were so close, I could barely contain my excitement. Though we hadn't been matched up with a child yet, we decided we would name our daughter Lillian Grace. She would be home within eighteen months.

Brittany answered the phone at the agency. Bibbetty Bobbetty Brittany, my husband and I called her because she was so young, so cheerful, so perky, and so very, very patronizing. She, in my opinion, was a necessary evil. "Mrs. Taylor, we're so glad you called. The Chinese government has just announced that they are changing their health requirements for adopting parents," she said. "Even though you've been medically pre-approved, we think you and Mr. Taylor should request a medical pre-approval again based on the new requirements. We can have the answer tomorrow morning."

My body tensed up, and I felt my stomach drop, but I quickly pushed my nerves aside and calmed myself down. *Okay. This is a shock, but everything is going to be fine because we are unstoppable.*

We have worked too hard for this, put four years of our lives into saving the money and gathering the paperwork. Besides, Brittany sounded as stupidly cheerful as ever—surely she would be more serious if there was really an issue. It simply isn't possible that this will stop us.

But it did. The next morning Brittany called and said in her usual cheerful voice, "I'm sorry, Mrs. Taylor, you and Mr. Taylor have come back likely to be denied." Suddenly we no longer had a plan. I couldn't think. I couldn't speak. I couldn't move. "Mrs.

What will we do now? I feel so lost.

Taylor, we can send your dossier anyway and see what happens," she added, still nauseatingly perky. Now, I was furious. I couldn't stand that patronizing bitch one more second. I was going to show her that I knew the facts. In my best teacher-to-idiot-student voice,

I asked, "And how much will that cost us? Don't we have to send ten-thousand dollars with our dossier?"

"Yes," she replied.

"And how much of that is refundable?"

She answered, "Well, none, of course."

I said, "Then I don't think we'll be doing that."

Before she hung up she said, "Okay, Mrs. Taylor. Let us know if there's anything else we can do to help you." I couldn't believe it. She was still as patronizing as ever. What did she know, anyway?

But I knew what she knew. She knew we weren't getting a baby. We had worked diligently to pay off fifty-thousand dollars in debt and save the money we needed to pay for the adoption. Finally, we had twenty-five-thousand dollars in the bank and the paperwork gathered. But now we had no place to send it. *What will we do now? I feel so lost.*

We had started our journey with Catholic Charities, through whom I was adopted and through whom I had always planned to adopt. Their response was unexpected: "We don't need any more white parents. We have too many. You'll be on a waiting list for two years, and then it will take three to five years to match you with a birth parent."

Okay. Time for a new plan. We explored every adoption program available, international and domestic. Our plan changed repeatedly as we were told: You're too old; you're too young; you're too fat; you haven't been married long enough; you can't have a closed adoption; you don't have enough money; you have to give the foster children back when we tell you to, even if you are attached. (I can't even give my foster cats back—there is a reason I have five.) But finally, we were told, "You're perfect." And we had a new plan: we would adopt a little girl from China. We announced our news to our families by giving each member a Chinese ornament

---

"An invisible red thread connects the hearts of those who are destined to meet, regardless of time, place, or circumstances. The thread may stretch, or tangle, but never break."

---

with a lovely red thread Chinese proverb attached: "An invisible red thread connects the hearts of those who are destined to meet, regardless of time, place, or circumstances. The thread may stretch, or tangle, but never break."

Now it seemed we had finally encountered an obstacle we could not knock down, climb over, or get around. After hanging up with Brittany, I explained the situation with our application to Rick.

"It's okay, honey," he said. "We'll just do Russia instead. Russia was our second choice."

Suddenly, I was hysterical. "No! My baby is Asian. I don't want some white, lumpy baby. I want my baby. My baby is Asian."

Rick said, "Weren't you the one who always said that you didn't care what ethnicity your baby is?"

"Yes, but I care now. My baby is Asian. I don't want any other baby." It was true. I couldn't explain it, and I knew it was ridiculous, but I knew with all my being that my baby was Asian, and I was sure that I had just lost her.

Very calmly, in that tone of voice people use when dealing with crazy people, Rick answered, "Okay, honey, you go lie down. I'll find us an Asian baby." Just like he'd say, "I'll find us that cereal." I know he was wishing he could also say, "You go take a Valium." Too bad we didn't have any. I would have gladly taken all the Valium in the world right then to end the bone-deep, cold despair inside me.

As the nanny carried Lily in, I wanted to rush forward and snatch my baby from her arms.

Rick turned to the computer. I almost reminded him that we didn't qualify for Korea, that Vietnam and Cambodia were closed to adoption, that Kazakhstan required too long a stay. There were no other possibilities of Asian children. I almost told him that it was okay, that of course I didn't have to have an Asian baby; we hadn't picked China because the children were Asian, we picked it because the program was a good one. I almost told him these things, but I didn't. I couldn't. I was too busy worrying about the gaping black hole inside me, the one that used to be filled with hope, and happiness, and a baby, and a plan, and was now so empty. With every second, I could feel it growing, sucking me into it. I knew soon I would disappear, and nothing would be left of me, only dark, dense sadness.

Rick spent hours on the computer searching. When he called me, I knew it was to tell me that he hadn't been able to find anything. I was fully prepared to tell him it was okay, even though it wasn't, because here was the man who loved me more than anything, who lived to make me happy, trying to do the impossible. I was shocked when he said, "We can adopt from Taiwan. There are only three agencies that work with Taiwan, which is why we didn't know about the program. They're closed till after Christmas. We can call then and see if we qualify. And remember, honey, there are other programs."

"Of course," I answered, but really I was thinking, *There are no other programs. I can't do this again. So many years, so much work on the paperwork, so much money already spent. We'll have to do it all again. I'm already thirty-eight. I just want my baby. God, how could you take away my baby?*

I went through the motions that Christmas. I couldn't talk about the adoption, just gave a vague answer whenever anyone asked how things were going. I couldn't speak of it because if I started speaking about it, I would start screaming, wailing forth my grief and rage, "My baby was stolen, my baby was stolen, my baby was stolen!" Once started, I could never stop.

But a glimmer of hope had been born in that dark place within me, and every chance I got, I locked myself in with the computer to study the beautiful faces of the waiting children listed for adoption in Taiwan, to fall a bit in love with each of them, and to wonder if one of them was my child.

After Christmas we called one of the agencies that worked with Taiwan. The woman we spoke to asked us a few questions. "You haven't been married long enough to qualify for the Taiwan program," she said. "You do, however, qualify for Vietnam."

What was this idiot talking about? Vietnam had been closed to adoption for three years. I couldn't believe the rudeness, the coldness, the hardness of my voice when I responded, "Vietnam's closed."

Unfazed, she explained, "Yes, but it's reopening again in the next month, and the paperwork is almost the same as China's. Are you interested?"

I knew nothing about Vietnam. But it didn't matter. *I just want a baby. I don't care what it looks like. I don't care if it's healthy. I don't even care if it has arms, legs, a head. I just want a damn baby!* "Yes. What do we have to do?"

Fourteen months later, Rick and I waited, anxious and excited, in a Vietnamese orphanage, for our first in-person glimpse of our daughter. In their all-metal rocking cribs with bamboo mats at the base, every one of the fifteen babies who shared Lily's room was gorgeous. I wanted to take all of them home. As the nanny carried Lily in, I wanted to rush forward and snatch my baby from her arms. That overwhelming emptiness, the one that had not left me completely since our Chinese adoption failed, was screaming to finally be filled. In all those months, I hadn't been able to quite fill that place with enough hope or joy to overcome the fear that I would never get my baby, that this day would never happen. I hadn't been able to plan, only take the actions required of me to get to this point, and I had felt very stoppable at each step of the way. I still felt stoppable, still worried that someone would snatch my baby away at the last moment. But here we were. I was about to get my beautiful, precious baby at last.

As the nanny started to hand her to me, I pointed to Rick. He should be the first to hold our daughter. He had made this moment possible, taking on the modern-day Herculean task of finding an Asian baby to adopt where none existed. Yes, Rick had brought this miracle about, and he deserved this first moment. That scared place inside me that still thought this might not be real could wait. As I watched Rick take our daughter in his arms, my fears disappeared. A rush of fierce joy flooded through me. This baby was ours forever.

That night, as we held the amazing miracle of our sleeping baby, unable to put her down just yet because she was so precious, I thought about the previous Christmas and my claim that my baby was Asian. "You are Asian, and I am so glad," I whispered to her. Finally, we put her to bed. Laying there in the dark, listening to her breathe, I suddenly realized that our little Lily would have been conceived right about the time that we were getting the news that our Chinese adoption was likely to be denied.

"Oh my God!" I thought, "You really were Asian, and you weren't lost, just someplace unplanned for." I found myself thinking again of the Chinese red thread proverb. I knew without a doubt that a thread had bound my heart to the heart of this baby long before we met.

Julia Taylor is a humorist, author, and speaker who specializes in finding the absurd, entertaining and hilarious in daily life. Through her company Life and Other Comedies, Julia helps others discover the humor in their own lives. Her books include Frisky in the Morning—and Other Tales of Sex, Seduction and Sleep Deprivation, *the forthcoming children's book* Somebody Change the Baby!, *and* Mama Drama *(2012 release). Connect with Julia at www.LifeAndOtherComedies.com.*

Elayne Kalila Doughty

From Brokenhearted to Openhearted

It's 1994; I am twenty-four years old, all alone in the melting hot city of New Delhi, India, and about ten thousand light years from home with six hundred dollars in my pocket. I have left everything behind—my flat, my friends, my job—in search of that "something" that has been missing as long as I can remember. My body feels itchy, dirty; I feel myself swelling, dripping sweat.

Everywhere I look, the streets are teeming with people living life on hyper-speed. Men bathing themselves under running faucets. Women in neon saris wielding pickaxes and digging the road. Cows chewing on cardboard boxes beneath flickering signs for Coca-Cola®. The whole world seems to be swirling in a grotesque carnival of images, upside down and inside out. I am dizzy, my heart is pounding out of my chest. The hot air is thick with soot, fried ghee and incense. It's too much, too chaotic. I have to get off this street. "Breathe. Don't panic, just breathe," I tell myself.

The next thing I know I am lying on a hospital bed with a drip in my arm. I am confused. Why can't I make sense of anything? I can't feel my body. It's as if I am floating above it. I am terrified. I feel as if I am being strangled—I am convinced I am dying. I have to get out of here. I have to find my way home....

A young Indian woman doctor with a bindi on her forehead leans toward me and says in a lilting voice, "Madam, you passed out at the bus station. You are suffering from cultural disorientation. This sometimes happens when you are far away from home." Even in my muddled state I muster a strangled smile; the irony doesn't escape me. It seems I've been far from home most of my life.

The seeds of this panic were planted a long, long time ago. Soon after I was born, my mum fell into a bad bout of postpartum depression, so bad that doctors wanted to send her away to recover. She did go away, and kept going away; until one day she went away and did not come back. I still remember what she looked like just

---

It seems I've been far from home most of my life.

---

before she left that last time, laying in bed, looking like half of herself, like a skeleton. I was scared, but I kissed her anyway and felt the pit of my tummy fall out, as if I were free-falling from a very tall building. I wanted to make her laugh, so I put on her high heels and stumbled around her bedroom.

When my dad said, "Mum has to go away again," hot tears ran down my face. Furious, I cried myself into exhaustion. I wanted to destroy the world. After she left I kept thinking, *Why did she leave me? Why?* And in a fit of fiery hot rage I made a secret vow: "I will never let her back in again. She can knock all she wants, but I will never let her in again."

The moment I made that vow, something in me broke. I think it was my heart. My heart shut, and with it all that it represented—love, safety, trust, a sense of home. Where my heart once beat strong and sure was a sharp, brittle, hollow feeling. And like grit within an oyster shell, the shards of my broken heart began to irritate me. Somewhere, deep down inside of me, an intense panic started to grow, followed by a feeling of not belonging, a feeling of not being real. These feelings grew and grew until it was like I was living outside of myself, not really there. I had no idea where home was.

The panic attack in India wasn't the first, and it wouldn't be the last. For years I traveled the world in search of something missing:

a deep need to find my way back home to my heart. During my travels I often felt an extreme sense of panic and fear that struck me frozen. At first I would have to retreat to the safety of a hotel room, close the curtains and sit very still, trying to make the chaos I felt inside stop. In those moments it felt like I was about to fall apart. Over time I found a way to calm myself; I imagined an image of the "Great Mother," the universal Mother who looks after all beings on the planet. She is tall, broad and strong, with arms that wrap around me and hold me tight and a calm, open, black face. When I feel her envelop me in unconditional love, I know that everything is okay. I still dream up this image of the Great Mother when I feel fear shutting my heart.

------

*I still dream up this image of the Great
Mother when I feel fear shutting my heart.*

It's 2007; I am traveling, yet again. I'm in Heathrow Airport, reading *Glamour* magazine, one of my secret guilty airport treats. As I flip though its glossy pages, promising me youthful skin, perky boobs and fuller lips, I stumble onto something totally unexpected. The typeface leaps off the page and slaps me awake: *The Women Who Are Dying and the Man Who is Saving Them*. It is an article written by my "shero," playwright and activist Eve Ensler.

I read it and receive as an onslaught Ensler's depiction of the horrific, grotesque genocide and sexual torture that is still, even as I write this, going on in Congo. When I finish, I feel like vomiting. I am literally shaking and crying as I see the that the wounded women spread across the pages of the magazine look just like my own image of the Great Mother. Beautiful, strong and black, they're dressed like birds of paradise, their long dresses and wrapped skirts vibrating with colors and patterns, heads wrapped with beautiful pieces of material tied in geometric shapes. They are regal, noble and sacred, and they are being tortured, raped and murdered.

For months I have vivid nightmares about the women in Congo, nightmares that wake me in a cold sweat and stay with me through my days. I am first overcome by grief, and then a state of heavy depression that lasts weeks. I feel immobilized and stuck. I don't know what to do. Then I become angry and irascible, indignant and filled with rage. Slowly I start to feel my heart breaking open, and I hear a soft quiet voice within me say, "When one woman suffers on this planet, we all suffer." Each day this voice within me grows

---

*I am surrounded by the faces
of the Great Mother.*

---

stronger until one morning I wake up with a strange sensation in my chest of light and spaciousness. I feel energy coming back into me, and a moment of intense clarity. I hear the voice of my own heart say, "We are all connected; every one of us is the Great Mother, and she is within every one of us." I turn to my sweetheart and simply say, "I've got to do something about this."

It's 2010; I am traveling again. Only this time something is different. I've just arrived at the Burundi airport on my way to Congo to run a program called *The Safe Embrace: Coming Home to Yourself*, a trauma-healing and leadership development training for women survivors of the genocide. I'm here to train them to help other women survivors recover from the terrible trauma and abuse they've experienced, but right now I feel like a scared little girl who has no idea what she's doing; it's midnight and the bus that is supposed to pick me up is nowhere to be seen.

I look outside and see groups of men, taxi drivers, buzzing around like mosquitoes. I know that I must not go outside; that would be really dangerous. I feel the old panic begin to rise, and I try to focus on the path that has led me to come to Congo; this lifelong search for a mother, for home, for my heart. I breathe and lean into the Great Mother, calling her arms to wrap me in love.

On day one of the training in Congo, we arrive at a run-down building with paint peeling off the walls, cracked windows and torn and tattered curtains. Behind desks all around the edge of the room sit the fifteen women who will be with me through the next eight days of training. They are quiet, eyeing me. Each one is dressed in vibrant colors: bright pink, bright yellow, heads wrapped to match. I am surrounded by the faces of the Great Mother.

I've moved mountains to be here, and here I am. I am here as a force of openhearted love. I am here to stand before my sisters and show them that we hear them; that they are not alone. I am here to hold space for the healing of all these women by holding space for us to remember what it means to be held by the arms of the Great Mother.

I invite them to sit in a circle with me; I see that they're primed for me to be the teacher, as if they're in school. We need to create a place where we are all women in a group with no leader, a place to define new possibilities for how to heal and create a culture of empowerment for women. We sit in a circle; I ask each woman to introduce herself. Some speak quietly with eyes cast down, others are direct and brief. We're breaking the ice.

Each day the ice melts more and more, and the frozen parts inside of us all begin to thaw. Smiles broaden; there's a wonderful kind of love in the room, healing all of us as we open ourselves to tell of incredible heartbreak. This golden light of love seeps into places in us that were previously untouched. "I've never shared this story," the women say. Not until now.

In this country where there is no safety, where so many have been terrorized out of their homes, we are finding a home in our hearts. We are finding a home in our shared smiles, in the touch of each other's hands, in the tears that salt our faces. Each day we end in the loving act of massaging one another, each woman anointing a sister with beautiful, aromatic healing oils. Each woman loves her sister back to life. Each woman becomes the Great Mother, unleashing a love so immense it can heal the world.

The night before I'm to leave Congo, I go back to my little room. I sit under the flickering light, exhausted. My body aches; I've been working day and night for two weeks. My hands still smell of lavender and rose. I've been healing, loving, growing and stretching; my heart feels tender, wide open. Something stirs deep inside me. I reach for my phone and dial. A voice answers in crackly static, "Hello?"

I answer, "Hello Mum. It's Lani." My body is flooded with a rush of tears as I reach out across the light years between us. "Mum, I am so sorry I've shut you out all these years. I'm so sorry I wouldn't let you in. I understand that you never really left. *I* was the one who left. I'm here now. Please forgive me." There's a pause on the other end of the line. I reach out across the light years with my heart cracked open. I lean back into the Great Mother and she holds me tight. In forgiveness, I come home to my heart. As my heart opens, I feel the vow I made so many years ago dissolve and the message of my mother, of the Great Mother, is clear: "I am right here. I have been with you all along."

———————

Elayne Kalila Doughty, MA, MFT, founder of The Queens of Transformation—Powerful Women Changing the World, The Soul Spa, and The Soulful Women Program, is a psychotherapist, author, speaker, soul midwife, ordained priestess and transformational coach. She has more than twenty years' experience working with the "Inner Pearl Process," where she expertly guides women to transform a painful past into a powerful present and an extraordinary future.

Elayne's transformational programs include "The Soul Detox Program—8 Guided Journeys to Cleanse Your Soul, Nourish Your Heart & Transform Your Life," "From Brokenhearted to Openhearted—How Painful Times Help You Grow" and "The Safe Embrace: 7 Steps to Healing Trauma and Coming Home to Yourself," a global program that promotes trauma healing and empowerment and actively seeds the vision of a world where women are respected and revered. Elayne is now implementing this program with Eve Ensler of The Vagina Monologues at the City of Joy in Bukavu, Congo (www.Vday.org). Connect with Elayne at www.ElayneDoughty.com.

Bret Warshawsky

The Hero's Journey

Fall of 1994: I am nineteen and in my first semester of film school in New York. Despite living with three good friends, I suddenly feel very much alone in the big city. All the women here are intimidating, spectacularly beautiful, like models. I can't tell if they're my age or thirty, and I certainly don't dare ask them out. I'm feeling a little depressed about all this, but it's nothing enormous or earth-shattering.

As Christmas approaches, I start having trouble sleeping. I've been reading *Zen & The Art of Motorcycle Maintenance* night and day, fascinated, obsessed. I'm living with fellow film students, and smoking a lot of pot, so no one notices anything unusual when I start talking a lot and more and more rapidly, spending money like crazy and still not sleeping. Day 3, Day 5, Day 6, not sleeping. Writing furiously in notebooks. Unable to focus, I cut classes and roam the streets listening to Nirvana.

I am due to take a trip to Italy for the holidays, and after seven days without sleep, I show up at my parents' house to get the plane tickets. The trip to New Jersey by bus is totally surreal. People's faces look strange. I spend the two-hour ride speaking with a rabbi about the Bible and listening to Led Zeppelin. The time passes unevenly, sometimes more quickly than I can account for. At other points I'm stuck on a bus to infinity. I get off on Route 9 and walk the mile to my childhood home. "Stairway To Heaven" plays in my headphones as I cross the highway thinking: *I will never die.* When I show up at home, my parents' reaction is strange. *Why are they looking at me like that?*

"You're acting very strange," my mom says. "Are you on drugs?" I protest, laughing, but then at midnight I wake my thirteen-year-old sister and break down crying and talking at her a hundred miles a minute. My emotions feel way too intense, and I can tell I'm scaring her, but I can't stop.

When I tell my parents, "Nothing can hurt me, did you know that? I could walk out into traffic right now and not be hit. Not a

---

When I show up at home, my parents' reaction is strange. Why are they looking at me like that?

---

scratch, I'm telling you," my dad says, "We're taking you to the hospital." I agree to it; I don't know why.

When we get to the hospital, I am separated from my parents and taken to a small white room, empty but for a video camera and two chairs, adjacent to the nurses' station. The nurse tells me, "Wait right here—a social worker will be in to talk with you in two minutes." And then she closes the door, and I wait. The two minutes go by and nobody comes. I feel totally agitated, wired and panicked, so I get up to leave the room. *Wait—it's been locked! I'm trapped.*

I start screaming. "Mom! Dad! Help me! They locked me in here!" I know they're sitting right there, but I can't see or talk to them. This is terrifying. Instead of someone coming in right away to hold my hand, say, "Hey, Bret, what's wrong?" and listen to me, they leave me alone in the room for half an hour. I start going crazy, hurling myself against the door, banging the walls with my fists, screaming and giving the video camera the finger. I am helpless!

When the doors open, what arrives is not help. They have nothing to say. Instead, they lead me into the hall and stick a needle in my arm. The pain is terrible, and instantly, I go into convulsions. *I'm dying!* I panic. *They're killing me! They're actually killing me right in front of my parents!*

"Mommy, Mommy!" I scream, "Help me, I'm dying!" I feel like a helpless little child. The nurse quickly administers another shot, and I go limp as quickly as I went into convulsions—peaceful, sure this will be the end. But it is an antidote, and the convulsions stop immediately. I look at my parents' ashen faces. My mother is staring at me. Her eyes are bewildered.

"He is psychotic and possibly a danger to himself and others," the doctors tell my parents. I am admitted to the psych ward against my will and placed in a sterile white room with nothing in it but a chest of drawers and two single beds. I am in shock. *What is happening to me? How can they just take my freedom away?* I punch the walls until my fists are black and blue, screaming, "Let me out of here! Why am I here? What are you doing to me?" My fear is primal and total. I cry like I have never cried before.

The doctors in the psych ward spend two weeks bringing me down from what they call "a severe manic or psychotic episode," though no one thinks to ask *me* what is going on. I am so confused—I swallow many different pills, and attend group therapy morning, noon and night.

I don't know what my real thoughts are anymore, and the overall atmosphere is simply bizarre. I hardly see my parents, and when they do come, they don't know how to treat me. The place is populated by frightening, intense people, all of whom seem completely lost to themselves.

The doctors decide that the next step is to send me to an inpatient clinic in Princeton: *So I am still to be imprisoned.* I ride there in an ambulance, and when we arrive, my parents meet with more doctors while I sit in the lobby, crushing my glasses to pieces against the tile floor and repeating, "I'm tired of seeing."

My emotions are on total overload. One moment, I feel I've seen the light of the world. The next, I'm terrified I'll be sucked into some vacuum of nothingness. I can't take it anymore.

When my parents come out, they announce: "The doctor thinks you're bipolar. We're admitting you to the inpatient wing for treatment." That's when I hear, for the first time, that I have a mental illness.

I feel complete bewilderment. And shame. Because of my now two-week-old comment about walking out into traffic, I am placed in the clinic's suicide ward, in a room with white brick walls. As a fan of the bands Pink Floyd and Nirvana, I have to laugh as I cry: *Oh my God—here's* The Wall *and they put me on "Lithium."* All day

---

I would have loved to have someone like me talk to me when I was twenty.

---

long I hear the incessant *click* of the air filter in the smoking room and the rhythmic beat of ping-pong balls in the recreation room. *Why would they put someone who's sensitive to sound and slightly paranoid between these two awful, clashing sounds?*

But I also find a saving grace: my roommate, Aaron. A Princeton student, he has just gone through a very similar experience to my own, and we share the absurdity of it all as we try to cope. He has kind eyes and a reassuring voice. My parents bring me a stack of books, including Whitman's *Leaves of Grass*. Aaron reads me passages from it in our room. I've never had a guy read me poetry before—it is intimate and caring in a way I'm not used to. I think we both save each other, during our first weeks in the clinic.

When I left the clinic six weeks later, I dragged a new and heavy self. My self-confidence, self-worth and self-esteem were totally destroyed; it was the first time I had ever experienced the devastation of the partner to severe mania—bipolar depression.

For the next ten years I was in and out of the psych ward six times; dosed with a variety of meds; deeply depressed; and addicted to marijuana, which brought on manic episodes every time. I lost the love of my life during one of these episodes—I told her, "I never loved you." It wasn't true, but I couldn't take it back. Regret and unrequited love plunged me further into depression and drug abuse—I smoked more pot to deal with the emotional and psychic pain. It was a vicious cycle, true insanity: smoking pot over and over again and expecting different results, only to end up in the psych ward again and again.

I was able to finally turn it around at twenty-nine, when I got sick and tired of being sick and tired—sick of depression, not having friends, being in the hospital all the time. One day I thought: *You have to quit smoking pot. And you have to take your meds. Do it for a year, and then reevaluate.*

It was the right leap of faith. Things slowly got clearer. I *could* be better; I could still follow my dreams. I started feeling excited about life. I'd been through it all in psych wards and in all those

---

The hero's return is in self-mastery, which is ultimately the freedom to live neither anticipating the future nor regretting the past.

---

programs that basically warehouse people. But when you're young, you don't want to talk about your illness, even though that's usually when you're diagnosed. You don't want to get help. It's a terrible irony. When a friend told me about a program of study in psychosocial rehabilitation, I wanted to be part of a new way of treating mental illness, to be part of a proactive, compassionate care I didn't get when I needed it most. I would have loved to have someone like me talk to me when I was twenty.

I realized that helping others was a path to helping myself. Revisiting Joseph Campbell, I realized that the hero's journey he describes was *my* journey; my odyssey down the rabbit hole of mental illness was a postmodern suburban vision-quest filled with magic, mysticism and initiation. The hero's return is in self-mastery, which is ultimately the freedom to live neither anticipating the future nor regretting the past. Looking at myself through a mythic lens, I realized slowly but definitively: *Experiencing a mental illness does not mean* being *an illness. It is not eternal punishment but a blessing in disguise. I'm a survivor.*

45

My journey now has taken me to become a filmmaker, speaker and mental health advocate. As I write my films and focus my attention on motivating children faced with mental illness, I realize that the depth and intensity of my time spent in the dark night of the soul was terrifying, but it did provide me with a kind of laboratory for self-discovery.

Coming back to life, like the mythic hero after his trials and tests, I have rich material and deeper understandings to transform into art and share with the world. I'm not my illness—I'm an artist with a unique and colorful past that breathes life and possibility into my future.

Bret A. Warshawsky is transforming bipolar disorder Into a blessing! He states: Welcome to the 21st century mental health reformation, transformation, evolution and revolution! We are here together to transform mental illness through allowing ourselves to follow our passions. Let's re-imagine and re-create how the world perceives mental illness and, more importantly, how those of us with these diagnoses perceive ourselves. A major component of this reformation is introducing alternative methods of treatment and recovery. Recover From nental Illness your own way— the paths are many—the Journey Is YOURS! Connect with Bret at www. BretAWarshawsky.com.

Elaine B. Greaves

The Miracle of Divine Timing

Like an animal of prey I scout the cafeteria hoping to secure lunch with perhaps enough food left over for an afternoon snack. Spotting success, I furtively move between tables, eyes downcast, and retrieve discarded packets of crackers my classmates have left behind.

Next I help myself to hot water, free as long as you bring a used cup and a teabag. I had paid for my first cup of tea that morning. With trembling hands I dunk the teabag, quickly remove it from the hot water and store it for later use. The tea and crackers help stifle my hunger pangs, tremors and nausea for at least a few hours. Then I make my way to my next class. I have performed this ritual, several times a day, every weekday, for almost three months. My shell-shocked mind no longer asks, *How much longer can I go on?*

I am at law school, in a foreign country, fulfilling a childhood dream. I still remember the sound of Portia's voice as Shakespeare's *The Merchant of Venice* played on my parent's radio. I had never heard a woman speak with such authority. I was in awe of her boldness and confidence and, at ten years old, I wanted to be like her. Being such a shy child, I thought, *If I could express myself like Portia, if I could speak for people who don't have a voice, that would be a miracle!* Having found my calling, I cried and went to my father and said, "I want to be a lawyer." I expected him to laugh.

Instead, he, with barely a third-grade education, embraced my dream. He said, "If that's what you want, we'll make sure it happens."

Thus began my journey. I attended the right college, took the right courses, applied and was accepted into the right law schools. Then, I met "Mr. Right," a man I'll call "Harry," at a cousin's wedding. He had the most beautiful brown eyes, a soft, curly Afro—it was love at first sight, for me. We talked. He seemed interested. It was a beginning.

Harry invited me to visit him in Toronto. Two weeks later, I did just that. By the end of our week together, he asked me to marry him. I was twenty-one years old, and I had never really dated. My father, the Jamaican patriarch, never allowed it. Almost finished with college, I was liberated with a newfound freedom. Harry swept me off my feet with little effort. Soon, much to my parents'

I am here, at law school, in a foreign country, fulfilling a childhood dream.

distress, I was planning to move from my home in New York to Canada, to marry a man I barely knew. I ignored my father's objections. Even his threats of ceasing all contact couldn't deter me. When I applied and was accepted to a Canadian law school, I thought, *Fate has smiled on me.*

When I stepped off the plane in Toronto, I searched the crowd for my fiancé. Harry was barely recognizable. His hair was unkempt, his eyes were bloodshot, and he looked as if he'd slept in his clothes. Abruptly, in the voice of a stranger, he said, "This was a mistake. You need to go back home to your parents."

At that moment my words dried up, my throat closed tight, my heart died. I wanted to make him understand, but instead the words that failed me raced through my mind. *I have nothing to go back to! I gave up everything to be with you. Acceptance to law schools in the United States, scholarship awards, family, friends. I walked away from my parents. I chose you! My father will never forgive me. I believed your promises: that we'd get married, that you'd take care of me, that you'd nurture my dreams.*

With unexplained anger, Harry drove me to his apartment, the one we had planned to share as husband and wife. As soon as we arrived, he turned to me and said, "You need to be out of here tomorrow."

I stuttered, "But I have no money." He urged me to call my father and ask him to buy me a ticket home and then left me alone in the apartment. *I burned all my bridges. I have nowhere else to go.*

That night was the first of many nights I spent alone, fighting insomnia and, when at last I finally fell asleep, fighting nightmares. The next day he returned, prepared to take me to the airport. I could taste my dream and that helped me find my voice at last. "I came to Canada for two reasons," I told him. "One, to marry you and the other to attend law school. The first reason is apparently gone. I'm staying for the second."

Late that night the phone rang. My desperate heart hoped for a reconciliation, but instead, I heard a strange female voice on the line. "Elaine, if you don't leave Canada, I will kill you." *Kill me? Kill me? Who is this man associating with? I don't know anything about him. I'm not safe here.* With shattered dignity and profound desperation I phoned Harry's brother, who reluctantly agreed to take me in temporarily. I soon shared the cramped apartment with him, his wife and their newborn. I knew they struggled financially, so I refused most meals. I couldn't eat. I didn't want to deprive them.

Despair and terror fueled desperate prayers. As I sought answers I recalled my father mentioning a nephew in Toronto. Finding his name in the phone book, I called the number. A motherly voice answered. Haltingly I explained who I was. My hope faded when she said, "I'm his ex-wife, five years now." But then she invited me to visit, and I eagerly accepted. I realized too late that I had no money to get there. My reluctant host pressed a twenty-dollar bill into my hand. I gratefully accepted his sacrificial gift which later helped get me to and from school.

When I met "Mrs. D" and her fifteen-year-old daughter, "Diane," I was reassured and soon mentioned my search for new accommodations. Since she knew my father, Mrs. D invited me to move in and share a room with Diane, thank goodness, at no cost. Her small apartment was a welcome port in the storm, but this did not last. Within days, Mrs. D's older daughter visited and made it clear that, because I was related to her stepfather, I was not

Despair and terror fueled desperate prayers.

welcome. Among other things, she accused me of eating meals her mother could ill-afford to provide. That's when I started scouring the cafeteria for leftover crackers.

I made sure to leave early and return late. I told them I was on a meal plan at school because having a roof over my head became more important than eating. Between classes I slept in the library. On weekends as I rode the subways, I studied and took cat naps. One subway token could take me any place I wanted to go as long as I didn't get off the train.

At night, hot, silent tears, yearning for family and fear of the unknown were my dogged companions. Yet that did not compare to the shame I'd feel if I had to return home with nothing to show for it. Life got worse. Diane took cues from her older sister, and I became the brunt of her daily bile. She complained about every move I made. The final eruption came weeks later when Diane's older sister again stopped by and loudly declared that she would no longer visit while I was living there. I had to be out in four days.

It's now Thursday. I walk across campus to forage for more crackers, and I feel an inexplicable urge to take a different route to the Student Center. As I follow the unfamiliar path I see a solitary figure in the distance. After puzzled looks and uncertain smiles, mutual recognition dawns, and the miracle of coincidences leaves me breathless. I see that it is Maureen. We had attended the same church in Jamaica some ten years before. We barely spoke as children, yet we now hug like long-lost friends.

"I bet my mother would love to see you," she says. *But her mother hardly knows me*, I thought as I dare to embrace yet another miracle. "Why don't you come by our house on Saturday?"

Knowing that on Saturday I would be homeless, I quickly blurt out, "I'll be busy on Saturday, but how about Friday?"

With the few coins left in my purse I set off the next afternoon to visit Maureen's family. I weigh thirty pounds less than when I got off that plane a lifetime ago, and my clothing hangs precariously on my weak frame. I carefully comb over the spots where my hair has fallen out due to stress and lack of nutrients. On the bus I again thank God for allowing me to be in school. I pray for a place to live, nutrition for my weak body and reconciliation with my family.

My heart swells with the power of dogged perseverance, the miracle of divine timing and the joy of answered prayers all along my path.

Maureen's home is the most beautiful home I've ever seen. It's warm and inviting, and love pulsates from every corner. Mommy H and her brood of five greet me. The hugs and kisses I receive are more than I can fathom. After the meal, I take the plunge. "I came today because tomorrow I'll be looking for a place to stay," I explained. "Do you know of any rooms for rent?"

"Why not stay with us?" Mommy H asks. "We have a spare bedroom."

Cautious joy wells up as I begin, "I don't have much money...."

Without hesitation, Mommy H says, "There's no charge. You'll be like one of my daughters."

My throat opens up, my heart comes alive and I weep uncontrollably. Mommy H holds me in her arms, soothes my brow with a warm towel and stays next to me until I fall asleep. In time she nurses my emaciated body back to health and with tender love and care helps me to repair my broken spirit.

My heart swells with the power of dogged perseverance, the miracle of divine timing and the joy of answered prayers all along my path. "Daddy, I'm sorry for my choices... I love and need you in my life...." Eventually, a heartfelt letter to my father brought about a reconciliation. "Our next graduate, Elaine Greaves...." Three years later, with dreams fulfilled, my parents watched me cross the stage to receive my Canadian law degree. My dream to emulate Portia from Shakespeare's work, to use my powerful voice to advocate for those without a voice, is now my reality. I have used my voice for decades, helping my clients go from feeling lost and powerless to feeling the presence of someone who really cares for them. My challenging time in law school has been my constant source for compassion and connection.

I now know that even when I'm in the midst of pain, despair and heartache, I can endure. I can find a way to climb over, tunnel under or push through any adversity that comes my way. Every time I bounce back from hardship or despair, I am reminded of the greatest gifts this experience gave me: resilience and the abiding belief in miracles. As a law school administrator, I am always mindful of the dedicated and resilient students who may just be looking for crackers and hot water as their daily meal.

Elaine B. Greaves is a motivational speaker and author of the book, A Season to Success. She is an attorney and has practiced law for decades. She earned a BA in political science from Fordham University, Bronx, New York, an LLB from Osgoode Hall Law School, Toronto, Canada, and an LLM from New York University School of Law. Elaine has helped thousands of clients navigate the legal system. As a college professor, then a law school administrator, she worked to have a positive impact on young people and motivate them to their fullest potential. President of Season to Success, Inc., she is a leadership and success coach and helps individual and business clients reach their optimum goals. She is the proud mother of daughters Brandeis and Mandela. Connect with Elaine at www.ElaineBGreaves.com.

Lyndsie Zacheis

Learning to Stand

"Do you know why I hate you?" My stepfather towered over me, his ice-blue eyes ringed by an unhealthy yellow cast, his pasty arms resting on his hips. His jaw began to tighten, waiting for my response.

I wasn't sure what to say. Did he really want me to say it? To name it, out here on the front porch, out loud to his face? Or was I being forced to play another game?

"Yes," I answered, avoiding his eyes, while tears ran from my own.

"Why?" He demanded as he leaned in closer. "Answer me. *Why?*" My back was pushed against the wall, while he caged me with his arms, one on each side. I was trapped in more than one way. I was just sixteen; it was dark outside and I was dressed only in my pajama top. Mom was inside, but what could she do? Last time she only looked on, frozen, expressionless in her rocking chair.

Time was up. He pursed his lips, and a moment later I felt his spit running down my face. Panic flared in my chest; no matter how many times he did this to me, it still hurt. I braced for the first hit. It came in the face—a slap, followed by a punch to my side. He was yelling now, "Why? Why do I hate you, Lyndsie?" And yet no one seemed to hear him shouting, no one from any house nearby. No one ever came to help me, to stop him.

"Because of what I make you think," I answered, as I doubled over to hug my new bruise. "Because of what I make you do."

That was the right answer, but it didn't stop the hitting. When I was about to fall over, he stopped abruptly and growled, "You wait here." I heard him go into the house and yell at my mother, "This time I'm getting rid of her." I froze. Where could I run? To a neighbor's? No, they never want to get involved. To church? No, they'd just send me home, as so many times before. And then it was too late. He was in front of me again.

"Get in the car," he ordered. I did, because if I didn't, I'd feel his hand or fist again. He took off with an angry squeal of tires

---

I braced for the first hit.

---

and began to drive, fast. I knew what this meant—his mood was really bad. Slow driving meant a good mood. I knew all of his tells by heart. Any child of an abusive parent does; it's our mode of survival.

Even though Mark was my stepfather, he was the only father I ever knew. Even though he always hurt me, I still loved him, and I wanted him to love me. Driving with his left hand, he used his right to keep punching me as he screamed, "You think you know hurt? Well, I'm going to beat you to death." We tore around a corner and for a minute I was thrown against the car door. I could see his face. He was serious.

I was only five years old when Mark first walked in our door. He had just started dating my mother, and had come to watch my brother Joshua and me while my mother was out. "You guys want to help me out?" he asked. "I want to make it real nice here for your mother." We eagerly did the chores as he instructed us, folding laundry, tidying up the pots and pans. We were so proud. But then he turned on us.

"Why didn't you let my dog out? Look at this mess." There was a pile of poop on the kitchen floor, and he shoved first Josh's and then my face into it. When he released us—humiliated, terrified and confused—he said in a steady voice, "There's an easy way and a hard way. You've chosen the hard way."

That night, I tried to tell my mother, but her answer wasn't what I expected. "Don't you ever say such a thing again," she said in disbelief. "He would never do that. No one would." And so began the many years of abuse, and the many years of bearing it—alone, I thought.

Mark and my mother married soon after they started dating. He was stern and angry. My siblings and I learned to walk on eggshells around him, but he always had it in for me in particular. One rainy day, I absentmindedly tracked mud on the floor. "Look what you did, Lyndsie," he shouted. "Clean it up. Now!" He grabbed me on the back of my neck and pushed me down by the cleaning supplies. I avoided his eyes. He was like a wild animal; you never want to look them in the eyes.

---

*I will never forget the first time
he came into my room.*

He dragged me into the dining room, and I had a little burst of hope. Mom was sitting in there. I looked at her with a pleading expression. I felt Mark punch me in the side. I kept hoping my mother would do something, but Mark held me by the hair, yelling, "You are so disrespectful! What do the scriptures say? What?!" I felt myself being lifted off the floor, and before I realized what was happening, I was in the air. I hit the wall so hard my whole body shook.

Then came the blood, from my nose. A drop hit the floor, and that set him off again. Finally, he forced me to crawl to my mother, to kiss her feet and ask her forgiveness for making the floor dirty, this time with my blood. She sat there silently. My mother herself was trapped and knew the power of his fists. I bent over her feet, feeling shaken, abandoned and completely alone.

I will never forget the first time he came into my room. I was ten, barely developing. I understand now why night is associated with darkness and evil. It was for me. Mark progressed from merely cupping my breasts, to forcing me to watch him touch himself, to touching me. He was disgusting. I hated his heavy breathing, his pasty white skin.

But a part of me still loved him, still wanted a father to take care of me, as any little girl would.

---

*In that moment, I began to
see myself as strong.*

Over the years, I came to feel less and less worthy of love. I prayed and wondered what was the matter with me. I believed all the abusive words he said. Why wouldn't I? Children don't stop to think that parents who are supposed to love, encourage and protect them might be wrong. I began to loathe myself, and act out at school—the one place I, not Mark, was in control. Bruises on the outside healed with time. But on the inside, my soul was losing its light.

One afternoon, a few weeks before I wound up in the car with Mark, I lay in my room, depressed. I heard Mark and my mother in a loud conversation in the hallway. "If we could just get rid of Lyndsie—" Mark was saying. "I hate her."

It hurt me deeply, even after all he'd done. As I cried, I prayed, "Heavenly Father, why have You let this happen? Why are You putting me through this?" I sobbed and wept, trying to keep quiet.

And through the tears I received a message, as if I heard a voice saying, "I am not putting you through this; I am helping you through this."

In that moment, I began to see myself as strong. I began to keep a positive journal, forcing myself every day to write down ten things that were good about me. On some days, it was really hard to come up with ten. I slipped back into depression occasionally. But I kept going little by little. I felt a burden of responsibility— maybe others were dealing with this pain, and maybe I could help them find a way out.

So when Mark had me in the car, I wasn't the same girl I had been just a few weeks earlier; I had begun to build a core of strength. Suddenly, he punched me. Then it was all clear: his hatred of me was born of his hatred of himself. It was him, not me; it was his shame, not mine. We approached the police station. He slowed down and I saw my chance. I jumped out. I found out later that he intended to kill me there and then turn himself in. He just wanted the final satisfaction of making me suffer.

I reached the door of the police station and froze, terrified. I didn't yet possess the strength to defy him, to open the massive, black iron door; I knew I'd be opening the door on the years of pain our family had suffered. I knew once I turned that handle, there was no turning back. Fear welled in my chest, crept up my throat. I ignored it, envisioning my journal and the ten good things I'd written that day. I began to recall each one, and imagined them as ten strong fingers on my hands. Then the door opened, by some force that didn't come from me alone.

Mark was arrested. He spent three years in jail, and was released on good behavior. He was dealt a blow of justice by his fellow inmates, in the form of a two-by-four to the head. I am not vengeful, but even to criminals, child molesters are the epitome of evil.

I realized that carrying the anger, the hatred and the fear would only continue to allow him to control me, so I forgave Mark. It was more difficult to forgive my mother. I had to place myself in her shoes, the shoes of a woman who searched for her own self-love, who felt just as trapped as I did and even more powerless. She is deeply remorseful and we are friends now. I am proud of our relationship, of whom she has become and what she, too, has overcome.

And I know that I made the right choice; I chose to stand on the rock of my hard experience, rather than sink into the sands of endless pain. I realize that the Heavenly Father was in fact helping me to get through my nightmare. My list of ten good things about me gave me strength to leap from the car; turn the handle on the police station door; testify; forgive myself, my mother and Mark and start a life of spreading an inspirational message of grace and possibility. I'm grateful to my Heavenly Father for the trials in my life that are now blessings.

Lyndsie Zacheis is an author and speaker who shares her triumphant story of survival and inspiring message with readers and audiences nationwide. She has been a regular guest on the radio program Salute America. Lyndsie is an author of fiction and nonfiction books. She also ghostwrites. She is currently writing her autobiography, Loving After Hating. Connect with Lyndsie at www.LyndsieZacheis.com.

Jacinta M. Higgs, EdD

Lifted Taboo

Six months after my graduation from college as a trained teacher, I got married at twenty-one to a wonderful, loving man who was my friend and confidante. I was experiencing life at the top of my game: I felt so deeply loved, enjoying a sense of security, peace, completion and hope. Dwight and I spent two beautiful years living in a state of honeymoon bliss, just loving each other. Then the intrusion and meddling began. People kept asking, "Any foot for socks?" In other words, when were we going to have children?

We had talked about children many times and wanted a stable financial base for our family first. But with all the community chatter and whispering as I walked by, my mind finally succumbed to the pressure. After trying and not getting pregnant, I began to think something was wrong with me. Deeply worried, I prayed and prayed to God for a child. Within six months we conceived, and nine months later Dwight and I became the proud parents of a beautiful baby girl, Cecilia Paulette. We were so thankful and happy, and the announcement and celebration of our precious gift echoed throughout our tiny island.

The deep joys of motherhood were phenomenally exciting, a whole new way of falling in love. And I did everything right—or so I thought. I breastfed my beloved Cecilia, sang to her, read to her, loved her with a fierce tenderness. I wept, marveling at the perfection of her tiny form, the quickness of her new mind.

But between the demands of motherhood and work, I forgot to care for myself. Day or night, whenever Cecilia slept, I spent hours writing notes and worksheets to send to school for my students, since there were no consistent substitute teachers for them while I was on leave, and they were preparing to sit for a national exam in three months. Though I had lots of help and support from Dwight and my family, I was anxious and barely slept; and because I was trying to lose weight, I didn't eat enough. It all seemed normal for a new parent.

On the morning I was to return to my work at school, I got up early to care for and dress the baby. Once Cecilia was ready, I laid her in her crib and began to prepare myself. As I stood in front of the mirror, combing my hair, I suddenly felt my body shake

It all seemed normal for a new parent.

uncontrollably. The vibration increased and my sense of balance disappeared. *Oh my God, what is happening to me?* Terrified, unable to cry out, raking the air with my arms as I fell backwards, I jolted violently into convulsing spasms and I lost consciousness.

I do not know, to this day, how long I blacked out. I awoke, dazed and uncertain what had happened, to Cecilia's crying. Feeling cold with shock, I picked her up and attempted to pacify her.

After medical observation and attention at the nearest clinic, I was given seizure medication and advised to go home and get rest. By that evening, the news had spread to my family and friends, and many well-wishers came by our home to visit. I welcomed the support because I was terrified to be alone. I was terrified to hold Cecilia. *What if I black out again while I'm holding her? What if the medication in my breast milk is bad for her? What if something is seriously wrong? What if I can't take care of my baby?*

By the next morning, my heart was so burdened with all these cares that I became deeply troubled, but the visitors continued to pour into our home. Then, in the midst of the crowded room, I felt my spirit running for deep inner cover as my control began slipping away into a second seizure. *Oh, no. Oh, God, please, no....*

Everything turned dark, and I heard my mother and aunts screaming, "Oh my God—Jacinta! Jacinta!" That was the last thing I remembered clearly for a very long time.

When I awoke, I found myself surrounded by old women in white gowns. Dwight told me I was in the ladies' ward of Princess Margaret Hospital. I felt like a zombie, greeting visitors without really understanding who they were.

Accounts from family members and friends describe how I talked "out of my head" and revealed secrets that I normally

---

That was the last thing I remembered
clearly for a very long time.

---

would have kept confidential. My thoughts became increasingly incoherent, my behavior unruly. My brother told me later that I kept bothering an elderly lady. "You thought it was our grandmother," he said. Eventually I became so agitated the staff restrained me, fastening me to my bed.

The doctors diagnosed my condition as a chemical imbalance: postpartum depression, complete mental breakdown. Not long after that, my mother called Dwight to say, "The doctors said that they cannot help Jacinta anymore and she must be committed to Sandilands." A mental institution. Being admitted to Sandilands as a mental patient has the most degrading stigma imaginable attached to it in The Bahamas.

Former patients are so horrified and devastated by the stigma that many of them allow the overwhelming embarrassment, pain and gossip to write off their possibilities for divine healing, progress, success and transformation.

Dwight was greatly distressed at the thought. "Miss Mackey," he said, "do not take my wife there. I need you to bring her home— here, to my house."

She said, "But Dwight, the doctors are saying Jacinta is very uncontrollable and they're afraid if we bring her home, something terrible will happen."

Dwight insisted. So doctors gave me extra drugs to make me sleep heavily, and I am told how my whole family kept a vigil at our home while amidst their prayers, I slept like a baby. Early next morning, before dawn, my family took me to a very small, elite, private mental institution, to evade the gossip spotlight.

My illness was the most horrifying experience imaginable for my entire family. When the news finally rang out that I was experiencing postpartum depression, my whole community was in shock. Fear and uncertainty filled the air, and rumors went viral. It was said that I had been hexed, that someone had fixed me with *obeah*. And I was only getting worse. Soon a third decision was made, to send me to an institution in Coral Gables, Florida. There, I received enough medication for two elephants and terrifying shock treatments. My memory of other patients and doctors' faces is blurred. But I remember the bright lights and saying, "No, no, no…" weakly, over and over again, as they administered the shocks.

A family friend visited me in the hospital. After he witnessed a shock treatment, he called my husband and said, "Man, you've got to get your wife out of there."

Dwight made immediate arrangements with my psychiatrist for me to be released to his care and took me to his family's apartment in Florida, away from the critical gazes and curious visits of everyone except my mother, sister and baby Cecilia. He patiently cared for me, held me, sat with me, talked with me and most importantly listened to me, incoherent as I was. And he slowly weaned me from the medication by reducing the amounts every other day. I have blurry memories of seeing him use a razor to cut tiny pills into even smaller pieces as we sat at the dining table. When I received a "You're good to go" prognosis from the doctor, I was elated but very frightened to return to The Bahamas to see my family and friends and most of all, my baby girl. *What if I fell apart again?*

Cecilia was baptized a few months later. I held her in my arms every moment I could, and we re-formed our interrupted bond, re-learning our love for each other. With time and family support, I healed, and the fun-loving, joyous energy of Jacinta Marie returned. The cares and concerns of being a new mother, a successful teacher, an active church volunteer, a community

---

I never allowed the unknowns, the fears, the embarrassment and the stigma of having a mental illness stop me from bouncing back.

---

leader and a dutiful wife challenged me greatly but were unable to puncture my unbreakable Khepera spirit—a spirit filled with the power and light of the sun.

The most difficult day of my life was my return to school. How would I face my coworkers and students? As I summoned strength to drag my feet of lead into the school, a little girl named Aneka saw me and immediately came running toward me with the most radiant, angelic smile. She flew into my arms, her little hands barely wrapping halfway around my full hips, and shouted, "Mrs. Higgs, we missed you so much!" I held her tiny body in that embrace of grace until her soul reached into the depths of my being and clutched onto my wounded soul. At once, my spirit sprang forth with rejuvenated zeal, and I knew all was well.

I was able to make it through that day, and the next, and the next. I cherished my relationships with my husband and family, I prayed myself to sleep, and I kept smiling, no matter what. Rebuilding my confidence, my broken memory and my faith in life was difficult, but I kept going, one day at a time. Sometimes I did not want to go on, but I still showed up. I never gave up. I never allowed the unknowns, the fears, the embarrassment and the stigma of having a mental illness stop me from bouncing back.

Three years later I became pregnant again and gave birth to a beautiful, healthy baby boy. Despite my fear, there was no replay of the postpartum depression. Twenty-one years later, I proudly stood in humble gratitude as Cecilia Paulette marched passed me in her graduation garb at Johns Hopkins University.

Today, I am so grateful for the understanding that what I experienced was not the taboo of an evil hex, as postpartum depression is often regarded in Nassau, but an all-too-common illness directly related to chemical and hormonal imbalance. The stigma around postpartum depression is still so strong, most women are afraid to talk about it. But my treasured hope is that, in reading this story, other women will find hope, the kind of emotional and medical support they really need, and the freedom from shame and taboo.

The Honourable Dr. Jacinta M. Higgs is President and CEO of Kem En Het Heritage Center, Principal of Akhepran International Academy, part-time faculty at the College of The Bahamas and Chairperson of the Clifton Heritage Authority—Bahamas. She is an Honourable Senator in the Legislative Parliament of The Bahamas government. Dr. Higgs was educated in the West Indies and at the University of St. Thomas in Minnesota, where she earned both her master's and a doctorate of education in critical pedagogy. She taught in the public schools for fifteen years and was awarded Teacher of the Year. She is also a former Director of Education and lecturer at Omega College and a well-known community activist, organizer and philanthropist who has written several self-published works, most recently her doctoral dissertation, which delineates how colonial education produced historical amnesia among African peoples. Dr. Higgs has presented papers all over the United States and the Caribbean. Learn more about her at www.JacintaHiggs.com.

Amanda Johnson

Upside–Down Messenger

My body felt at least one hundred pounds heavier as I struggled to hold it upright at the VIP table. *Three hours, Amanda. You can hold it together for three more hours.* For the first time in a long time, I felt lost again.

I looked around the room full of excited entrepreneurs who were making a living doing what they loved, and the lump in my throat grew.

I am supposed to be one of them! I was one of them, and it was the most inspiring work I've ever done. And people were saying YES—until the market crashed.

All the magic and miracles that had occurred in the last three years suddenly meant nothing. I was heartbroken and tired to my core. *How can I be feeling this way again, after all this work?*

"And thank you, Amanda Johnson," the happy voice snapped me back to the present and I smiled on cue, "for helping me restructure my book. You're a genius!" I nodded in gratitude for the generous acknowledgment, while my heart swelled with pain. *You were the first angel to help me. I don't have the heart to tell you it's falling apart AGAIN.* My stomach lurched at the thought of looking into her eyes and telling her that I had to walk away. *She'll be so disappointed.* I looked down and took a long deep breath to keep the tears at bay.

Just before the break, I escaped to the bathroom. If one more person asked me how I was doing, I was gonna lose it. Closing the stall door behind me, I clutched my head and let a few tears fall. *I can't believe this door is being slammed in my face too. It was so magical. The message came through. I set my intention, knowing that a secret teacher would show up. And she did. I believed the*

---

*I looked down and took a long deep
breath to keep the welling tears at bay.*

---

facilitator program was the perfect next step. And they accepted me. I've stayed the course in spite of the discomfort. I've served in every room, telling the stories I never intended to share. I've healed relationships, I've pounded pavement to showcase the program, I'm almost certified, and I had big contracts ready for signatures.

But now it doesn't matter. The organizations won't return my calls. All this work… for nothing. I understood they were cautious because of the market crash, but what about *my* dream of changing lives for a living?

When the music stopped in the ballroom, I wiped the mascara trail off my face and went back to support my friend. Walking into the room, I was overwhelmed with the energy of inspired entrepreneurs, and my heart sank again. *I am supposed to be one of them, but the bills are late and the account is empty… there's no other way.*

What about True to Intention? The still, small voice intruded over the excited activity.

What about it? I responded sarcastically. Six months earlier, I'd been inspired to change my business name and take it in a new direction. "True to Intention" resonated, capturing the message that had led me to Lisa and been confirmed over the past two years: *We come into this world with purpose (intention) and have everything we need to fulfill it—like the caterpillar has everything it needs to become a butterfly. But something happens, and we stop believing in those dreams that were placed within us. Our work is to remember our intention and be true to it.* The truth of the message was undeniable.

Once I said "yes" to my purpose, Lisa walked into a Sizzler behind me just three months later. In every teen workshop we facilitated, transformation occurred when kids realized they already have the power to change their lives. And the testimonials from my authors always went something like: *Thank you for helping me stay true to my real message.* True to Intention felt so right to me. I had to get this message out. And yet something was holding me back.

"You know, Amanda…" It was the last break of the day, and I'd mentioned my dream to a few friends again. One of them, obviously tired of hearing about it, said, "I think you should ask yourself why you're all talk. It's a great idea. Where are the business cards?" Her voice was full of love, but razor-sharp, and it cut through me.

Silently, I turned on my heel and tore out of the building, racing to get to my car before the dam broke. *You're never going to get yourself together.* I stumbled across the parking lot and struggled to steady my hand to unlock the door. *You're such a disappointment.* I

Struggling for my next breath, I asked myself if I should even bother.

---

sobbed all the way home. *Your family will starve because everything you do falls apart.* I got into my pajamas, turned off all the lights, and collapsed into bed. *You're a fraud—wait till everyone finds out! They thought you were bound for greatness, and look.* The venom flew at me with force, and I covered my head to shut out the voices.

Burying my wet face in my pillow, I screamed at God. *Why is this happening again? Why would you give me a message, put the people in my life to make it happen, and then take it all away again? Of course I don't want to move forward with my dream because the others were taken away! Every single one of them—teaching, online instructing, editing and now this! And as far as I can tell, it's YOUR fault! You opened the doors, and then you let them slam! Where have you been?*

Struggling for my next breath, I asked myself if I should even bother. What was I doing in this life? *Oh no! I am a fraud!* Here I was, ready to be certified to teach teens how to fall in love with themselves, and I was asking myself if I should keep on living? The room swirled, and the pressure in my chest grew. *You don't deserve to live.*

Pull it together, Amanda. You have a husband, a little boy, and a family to live for. You can't leave them behind. Pull yourself together! As soon as I asked myself the question, *How,* I remembered a tool we teach the teens. I reached for my journal and, cocooning myself with blankets, I started to write. "My negative self-talk

---

Relax into your upside-down
like the caterpillar does.

---

tells me that I'm worthless, that nothing will ever change, that I'm a disappointment, that I should just give up. It tells me that I'm a fraud, that my broken dreams are my fault, that I'm not good enough to have them."

I trembled as years of pain coursed through my veins, out through the pen, and onto the tear-smeared paper. I took a deep breath, silencing my resistance to doing what I knew I had to do next. I wrote: "My powerful self-talk tells me that I have a beautiful family to live for, that I have purpose and am worthy of my dreams. It tells me that I am a good mother and wife, that I am an incredible teacher who inspires, that I have a message and tools to help others. It reminds me that I have manifested miracles, that I have already made a difference, and that I have always been taken care of."

The venomous voices silenced, I heard the still, small voice within say: Amanda, do you see? All of those broken dreams you have taken on as failures? They weren't failures. You're using your teaching skills every day (just not the way you expected); you're inspiring others to be better versions of themselves through your work (just not the way you expected); and you're living your message in your parenting, marriage and career (just not the way you expected). And now, you're going to use the transformational training you've just completed (just not the way you expected).

The dreams didn't end because you weren't good enough or did something wrong. They ended because you got what you needed from them, and you needed to move to the next thing so you could do the work I have for you. I never abandoned you. You just didn't recognize me. *I WAS all of the closed doors*, directing you to be true to your intention and to help others be true to theirs. Beloved, dare to dream again. And lean into the discomfort. Relax into your upside-down like the caterpillar does. Trust that the transformation will happen—because it's meant to.

I picked up the phone and left a voicemail for the angel who was probably wondering where I'd disappeared to: "Hey, Sis. Sorry I had to leave. Can you call me Monday? I need to talk to you about a dream."

Amanda Johnson, founder of True to Intention, is a transformational speaker, author and messenger coach who supports aspiring authors in becoming the messengers they were destined to be. Trained by some of the world's most outstanding educators, powerful transformational coaches and heart-centered business experts, she's created a program that is designed to help aspiring authors clarify their message, write and publish their books and launch sustainable businesses in twelve to twenty-four months. In the last twelve months, many of her authors have significantly increased their brand integrity, loyalty and profitability simply by clarifying their message, connecting it with their purpose and saying "yes" to those next steps, the ones that always make themselves known. All this is done retreat-style, since Amanda is committed to giving her authors everything they need to thrive in their purpose and deliver their message to the readers, the industries and the world they were meant to transform. Connect with Amanda at www.TrueToIntention.com.

Skyler Madison

Reflections in a Mirror

"Good morning… Smiles… I am writing to you from across the ocean. Smiles… Please call me if you would like to talk. Alex de R…" Gloucestershire, England.

There was no profile or picture. I had met many nice people on the Internet dating site, but no one with whom I felt a real connection. The brevity of the note and the fact that he was from England made him intriguing and I emailed back my number, inviting Alex de R. to call me at my office. A day later he did, and I still remember the details vividly. My secretary ran into my office saying someone named Alexander de Rothschild was calling from England. Our initial conversation lasted for over an hour.

It was the beginning of an intense relationship in which we spent hours at a time on the phone. He, a retired investment banker, was going back to the London Business School to get a second PhD. He immediately told me he was not interested in a long-distance relationship, and had been thinking of relocating to the States. He was in a position to set up residence and complete his studies at either Columbia or Harvard.

When I asked what attracted him to me, he said my profile came up with a search using the terms "intelligent" and "educated." I had described myself as "sexy, smart, sophisticated and sane." Okay, that made sense, but what was a de Rothschild doing on an Internet dating site? His answer was plausible: He was the illegitimate child of one of the de Rothschilds. He was eccentric and shy. He liked American women, and his professor had encouraged him to get a life and try online dating. So here he was.

His voice and manner of speaking sounded as upper class as it gets. He suggested it would be more romantic *not* to show me a picture, that I should use my imagination instead. He described his looks as half Asian and half European, a cross between a well-dressed Mel Gibson and Jackie Chan. He seemed to know more about designer labels than I did. He was younger by four years; he drove a black BMW 6 series convertible; his favorite place was the South of France; he lived in the Cotswolds and collected sculpture and landscapes.

It sounded too good to be true, and when I said as much, he responded, "Why? Do you not think you deserve this?" Good question. If you had asked me, when I began my working life, if I would ever end up in a profession that involved helping others, I would have thought you were joking. Back in the 80s, when it was said that greed was good, the only one I was focused on helping was me, and the only things that mattered were making money and what money could buy. When I was not earning money on Wall Street, I was spending it shopping at Louis Vuitton, Gucci and Chanel. Making money and having more material possessions were my addictions.

But when I got the message from Alex de R., I had been immersed for seven years in my business, helping people change, and working hard on changing myself. After my divorce in 2000, my first transformational experience came through working with a Native American shamanic healer in St. George, Utah. I was put in touch with a wise, divine voice. During that experience, I asked why I wasn't finding love again. I was told I would have to be patient. I was changing so fast that, unless I wanted to be married and divorced several times, I must wait. It would come in due time.

So I waited. In 2001, I started a Center for Well Being in New York City, which was meant to be a place where people could not only focus on losing weight and changing unhealthy lifestyle habits, but also on cultivating their inner beauty and confidence. In the years since my divorce, I had learned from some wonderful meditation teachers, whom I believed helped me to clear my "love karma." So I was in a state of positive mental expectancy about meeting someone wonderful. Still, I waited.

And then he was there. Alexander and I began what I thought was an extraordinary adventure: falling in love without ever having met. He was right. Leaving the visual up to my imagination was very powerful. I knew what he smelled like because we both

---

*He had it down and knew exactly
what a woman wanted.*

---

wore the same scent (Hermes Eau D'Orange). Our conversations gave me access to his mind; it seemed deep and intense, revealed in hours of conversation that included discussions of philosophy and spirituality, from Alexander Pope to Marcus Aurelius.

I loved the sound of his voice. People in love often report that feeling. Soon the potent change in brain chemistry that love brings on made it impossible for me to wait another minute to meet him. After years of warning my children not to meet people online, I set up a rendezvous for the third week in June, three months after our first talk: a weekend at the Ritz.

Waiting for the British Airways flight to arrive, I wondered how I would recognize him. "You'll know," he had said. I recognized him by the extraordinary amount of Louis Vuitton luggage he was sporting. Alexander was, as he promised, Asian-looking with tanned skin and distinguished gray hair. The way he dressed was out of a magazine. There was an incredible gentleness to his nature that was intensified by his polished politeness.

The weekend we spent together was seamless. When I asked him what he fancied, he said he wanted to have breakfast at Tiffany's and for us to just be and explore the area, perhaps pop into the Ralph Lauren store. We walked together joined at the hip, holding hands and feeling as if we had known each other forever. I thought it amusing that it took him only a half hour of shopping to drop $3,000 on linen shirts at Loro Piano. During that time, frantic calls came in from my mother, trying to make sure I was not in the hands of a serial killer. Alex handled her beautifully. He was the master of charm; speaking with him calmed her concerns. "Will you grant me permission to court your daughter?" he asked.

He had it down and knew exactly what a woman wanted. The way he dressed, talked, and looked was, to me, simply fabulous. Clearly, he was tapping into the superficial part of me that I thought I had overcome. Despite the work I thought I had done on myself

---

Until that time, I had never
caught him in a lie.

---

to loosen my attachment to desires and materialism, I was wildly attracted to him. I went to England twice that fall. By the summer of 2007, all of his prize possessions had been shipped to my garage, and he was living with my family and me in Chappaqua.

We spent a blissful summer together. He came into work with me and helped on some of my writing projects. Weekends were spent doing absolutely everything together. We had so many common interests, and never got tired of one another. People at my yoga studio thought he was my guru. We read *Conversations with God* to each other every night. For complicated reasons he tried to explain, his assets in England were frozen, and before long I was loaning him money on a regular basis.

Soon after New Year's Day, 2008, someone to whom I was about to recommend him for a position in a hedge fund Googled him. Stories had just begun to break in the United Kingdom about how a woman named Christine Handy had been duped by Alexander; she lost over a million dollars. The articles called him a con man and a fraud. He had wooed her, sweeping her off her feet, promising to marry her and move to Switzerland to start a new career. She fell in love with him, funded his stay at London Business School and gave him money to invest for them. Instead, he used the money to buy all the toys he had when I met him: the BMW, the watches, the Dunhill pens. He cleaned her out and vanished, leaving her with piles of empty shopping bags.

The articles that began to surface in England alluded to other frauds. Alexander was not a de Rothschild, never went to Oxford or Eton, and made a career of scamming women, governments, literally everybody. Of course, Alexander managed to convince me

---

I would not let his betrayal define me. I would not be the victim.

---

that none of what the papers printed was true. It was not my habit to believe newspapers, anyway. He had me speak to his family in England, who told me Christine was crazy, and out to destroy him because she could not have him. Besides, hadn't I waited patiently for this love? I deserved all of it—the romance, the fairy tale, the adoration, the dream. That was the hardest part, the shattering of some dream.

Several days later, there was a loud knock on the door at 6:30 in the morning. I opened the door to an entourage of Immigration Enforcement officers, the FBI and local police. They wasted no time in handcuffing Alexander and escorting him from my home. He was allowed to take nothing to the detention center. He was to be deported to England and arrested upon arrival. The shock felt like a blow to the stomach. But I still wanted to help him, and so I was determined to get him out. Until that time, I had never caught him in a lie.

My two visits to the detainment facility seemed to be with someone I had known as Alexander, but who had become someone I did not recognize—Marc Hatton (which I believe is his real name). It was as if he had taken on a different personality. People were calling him a psychopath and sociopath, a confidence trickster who could charm anybody. He was as good as they get. But in that moment, in that room, all I could see was a sad, wounded man.

I wondered what had been done to him for him to end up this way. Perhaps I should have been angry, but I just felt sorry for him. Years of meditation and practicing non-attachment had prepared me for this moment. I would not let his betrayal define me. I would not be the victim.

The last time I saw him, I stared at Mr. Hatton, a prisoner in an orange jumpsuit. All the things he had sold his soul for were now sitting in my room: the shoes, the clothes, the pens, the computers, you name it—all of his precious stuff that meant so much to him. He said, "I am sorry if I hurt you."

I replied, "You didn't hurt me—it hurts because this was never love." I got up to leave, and thought about how he had violated all the principles I stand for: non-harming, truthfulness and a striving for non-attachment. What was I doing with him? I said to him calmly, "I hope you are prepared for the consequences of your actions. Have a good life."

Love is a powerful force. It can be a mirror, just as life is, to reveal to you who you really are. All love, whether it is of truth or deception, can be an opportunity for transformation. Despite his betrayal, I chose to view the experience with Alexander in a positive light, as a learning experience. I could easily have played the victim and been wounded for the rest of my life. Instead, I chose to see it as opening the possibility of loving passionately, even if it was a con. Ironically, I believe the lesson gained from how I dealt with that falsehood eventually allowed me to find the real happily ever after.

Skyler Madison is a motivational speaker and the creator of the Nirvana Diet. A certified hypnotherapist and wellness coach, Skyler opened one of the first wellness centers in New York City fifteen years ago. She holds an MA from Columbia University and is a PhD candidate in depth psychology. Her book, Material Buddha, *will be available soon. Connect with her at www.SkylerMadison.com or www.NirvanaDiet.com.*

Dana Rosser

Risking a Life to Save It

My husband, Butch, is lying flat on his back on a hospital gurney, about to be wheeled out of the room for gastric bypass surgery. I'm remembering the good times we've had. His Cheshire-cat smile that captivated me the first time we met is now a humble grin as he whispers, "Dana, this is the right thing to do." If the surgery, God willing, succeeds, we will have a fresh start in life, but the realization that he could die is unbearable. I'm terrified of being abandoned; I'm terrified of being left to raise our children without him. He looks up at me, "Dana, I love you and I'm doing this for us. I need you to be strong. Please just pray for me."

I nod, whisper, "I love you," and release his soft, tender hand.

The attendants wheel him away, the double doors swing shut behind him, and I stand there in disbelief. *Could I have done something to prevent this operation? Was there another weight loss option I missed?* For the next three hours, I sit in the waiting room, where I can't stop crying a river of tears.

I met my husband in Akron, Ohio. He was idolized somewhat like a god and considered one of the most successful laparoscopic surgeons in the world. He stood 6'4" tall at 450 pounds, which probably would have intimidated most, but it didn't intimidate me when I met him. I guess I could feel his heart from a distance. Plus, I thought he was cute!!

I had noticed that he was always hanging around in the hall after church, but I didn't think anything of it. Then one Sunday he said, "Excuse me, may I ask you a question?"

I said, "Sure!" *What could he possibly ask me that he doesn't already know?* I thought.

But he said, "I have a problem. I eat alone a lot. Do you ever have that problem?"

I said, "Yes, sometimes I do eat alone."

He said, "Well if you're eating alone and I'm eating alone, maybe we should eat together sometime." I thought, *boy that was a really smooth line.*

Our first date was at one of Butch's favorite restaurants. I arrived early; I told the hostess that I needed a table for two and that I was meeting Dr. Rosser. As I headed for a booth, the hostess gently said, "I think Dr. Rosser would be more comfortable at a table." Suddenly I felt anxious and ill-equipped to understand the

---

I'm terrified of being abandoned; I'm terrified of being left to raise our children without him.

---

sensitivities of someone who was morbidly obese. But from the time Butch stepped into the restaurant, we hit it off, and he immediately eased my fears. We ordered shrimp linguini, laughed and talked like we had known each other for years. We had planned on a movie too, but we were so caught up talking, we never made it.

We saw each other for close to a year before I realized I had fallen in love with him. I remember the day I knew he was the one. He called me to say he was on his way to pick me up for an outing. My mom was there; I hung up the phone and dropped onto the couch as if I'd been hit with a stun gun. I got this warm feeling in my heart; I couldn't wait to see him, couldn't wait to be with him! I turned to my mom and said, "Mom, I really, really love him! I've fallen in love with him!"

I grew up with a single mother who taught me to always be able to take care of myself, so the implication that I was a gold digger dating Butch for his money was hurtful. People didn't believe I could find a 450-pound man attractive; it had to be the money and status that was associated with him. I was doing very well before I met Butch; I had a great corporate sales job that allowed me to live very comfortably.

In spite of the naysayers, our commitment grew stronger. Butch and I decided to go through pre-marital counseling at church to make sure this relationship was what God wanted for our lives. Butch was divorced with three kids; I had my own issues. All of us have baggage going into a marriage, but I wanted to try to drop off at least two bags before we tied the knot. I don't think a gold digger would have done that.

People acted as if I couldn't see that Butch was morbidly obese; they treated me as if I were Helen Keller, deaf and blind. They would look at me as if to say, "Oh, you poor girl. What is a beautiful woman like you doing with him?" I saw beyond his outward appearance and zeroed in on his heart. I've dated men who were incredibly handsome and fit, but Butch's character and integrity made him very special in my eyes. Butch is a gentle soul filled with youthfulness, laughter and intelligence, a Southern gentleman to the core. His healing hands are a work of art, the most perfectly delicate soft hands I have ever felt. He adored me and I him. I felt his unconditional love for me daily and that was all that mattered.

Going into the marriage, I knew we would have to face the weight issue head on. Loving someone who is morbidly obese or "nutritionally challenged" sometimes feels like a silent hurricane stirring in your soul with no place to land. I was dedicated to helping him. I would see him eat terrible foods, but I didn't want him to think I was judging him. Butch headed up the laparoscopic center at Yale University, yet people constantly judged him based on his size, not his talent or abilities. I did not want to fall into that category. Home was a safe haven for Butch, a place where people didn't gawk at him and loved him unconditionally.

I wanted so badly for him to see that this behavior was killing him. Fried chicken and pizza were his go-to foods under stress, and I'd ask, "Are you really hungry? I mean, really?" and he would say, "I had a taste for it," which meant he was not hungry at all. When we became pregnant with twins shortly after our marriage, I was so excited, but the threat of Butch's health declining was constantly on my mind; fear of having to raise the babies on my own haunted me. Every time the phone rang I was afraid someone was calling to inform me that Butch had died of a heart attack.

Butch was blessed; he had no major illnesses, but I knew it was just a matter of time before he could develop diabetes, high blood

He adored me and I him. I felt his unconditional love for me daily and that was all that mattered.

pressure or heart disease. Since I didn't share my fear for his life with anyone, stress and eventually depression took center stage. My life got smaller. It seemed like I was losing Dana.

Slowly I started to become reclusive like Butch. I wanted to be close to Butch, and staying at home seemed safer. Living near New York, I often wanted to attend Broadway plays and concerts or have dinner with friends, but I knew that the seating at the venues were always going to be too small to accommodate Butch, and he wasn't too keen on socializing because he believed people judged him.

I could talk to no one about my true feelings for fear of being judged. Whom could I tell how sad, lonely and distressed I felt when he couldn't fit on rides at Disney World with the girls? Or how mortified I was when he leaned back in his seat on a plane once and it broke? He ended up in the lap of the person behind him, and there I was in the seat next to him, once again hurt and, yes, embarrassed. That word "embarrassed" was like a knife in my heart. I would never, ever say that. I never wanted him ever to know that I felt that way. I thought if he knew, it would crush his world, and the last thing I wanted to do was hurt him.

The low point came when were in South Africa for a conference where he was a keynote speaker. We were totally jetlagged, but we had to hurry up and get dressed for dinner. Butch was in the bathroom; I was on the bed trying to take a catnap. I heard a crash and a scream. *This is the heart attack!* I jumped up, ran into the bathroom and saw the toilet broken into pieces. He was lying there looking up at me with this expression that said, "Please help me."

I told him in the bravest voice I knew, "It's okay. We're going to go downstairs and tell them what happened."

The hotel staff was so accommodating; it was like we'd broken a glass or something, but I just wanted to cry inside. The humiliation was overwhelming, and then the enormous guilt from even thinking about myself. Still, I couldn't help thinking, *What about me? This is hard for me too.* That was my turning point. I finally realized I needed to start focusing on myself; I couldn't keep neglecting my own feelings. I started talking with a counselor. I started exercising. I signed up for art and cooking classes. I started

---

"I have to risk my life to save my life."

---

having lunch with friends. Slowly, I started taking better care of myself, and surprisingly, Butch noticed. "Could I come with you on one of your walks?" he asked.

My heart jumped the way it had the first time he held my hand. I smiled and said, "Of course, sweetie." I was a better person to be around because I found Dana again. I realized I had to be whole first if I was going to help anyone.

When Butch saw the progress I was making with my physical and mental health, he realized he really wanted to be here for us. He adored me and I him, and he simply wanted to live. His decision to have weight loss surgery was one that I will never forget. That was when he said: "I have to risk my life to save my life."

Now here we are: Butch the god-like surgeon, helpless under the knife, and me his loving wife, praying for one more chance to tell him I love him. My prayer is a mantra I repeat: *Please God, just let him live.* Through tears, I finally see Dr. Phil Schauer enter the waiting room. He says, "Dana, Butch is okay, he did fine."

As I walk down the long hall, I feel so grateful to witness the new birth of my husband. I kiss him, "I'm so proud of you. I love you. God was smiling on you. I'm here for you, whatever you need."

After the surgery, Butch lost quite a bit of weight. Our quality of life improved tenfold; we've done things we could only dream of, including para-sailing! Recently he ran a 5K with the twins and my sister, Dawn, while I ran a half-marathon. I cried while I ran; I was thinking: *My husband is running! He's running three miles!*

Butch said to me that day as he laid on the gurney on his way into surgery that he wanted to give our family a fresh new start. He asked that I pray for him, and I prayed for God to just let him live. I never imagined that a fresh start would feel so good and that living could be this breathtaking. Close to the finish line, I could hear my family screaming my name. As I crossed the finish line and ran into their outstretched arms, I knew that I had won so much more than a race; I had won my family back.

Dana Rosser has created a website dedicated to the issue of obesity; her goal is to create a space for dialogue and support for people with obese spouses and loved ones. She has written articles on the subject of obesity and relationships, and she and her husband, Dr. James "Butch" Rosser Jr., have lectured at the National Medical Association (regional & national), Harvard Patients Safety and Obesity Surgery Conference and the American Academy of Family Practitioners Conference about this delicate subject. Dana's forthcoming book Thru Thick and Thin, Facing Obesity through the Eyes of a Loved One, *will be released in 2012. Connect with Dana at www.FacingObesity.com.*

Dawn-Marie Hanrahan

On Grief and Grace

My young children—Amy, six and Matthew, eight—had never seen me so distraught. They had heard me cry before, but not like this, and not for so long. I sat on the edge of Matthew's bed, holding his hand because I needed to have a long-overdue, emotional conversation with my son.

It had been four days since we received that life-shattering phone call from New York, three thousand miles away in Washington State. "Hi, Dawn," a faint but familiar voice had said when I picked up the phone. It was unusual for Michael, my best friend Linda's brother, to call me before seven a.m., and by the tone in his voice, I knew something was wrong.

"Is it Mom? Or Dad?" I asked suddenly realizing if there was bad news from back home about their parents, Linda would have called, not Michael.

"No, it's not Mom or Dad." Michael's voice quivered, "it's Linda." Graphic pictures exploded into my thoughts. Car wreck? Biking accident? How bad were her injuries, so many horrific possibilities and then it came... "She died."

My breath and blood withdrew. My hands and feet turned icy cold and I began to shake uncontrollably. I was not ready to hear those words. I was not ready to have her gone. It didn't make sense—we weren't finished with life, with our dreams, with our friendship. We were only thirty-five years old. We had been best friends, sleep-over buddies, pinky-swear-secret-keeper girlfriends for twenty-eight of those years. We were the "other" daughter in each others' families. She can't be dead. Don't let her be dead, I silently prayed. "What happened?" I sobbed.

Michael explained the entire family had gathered the night before for a reunion with relatives visiting from Italy. "Linda was so happy," Michael said. "She told everybody about the good news from the adoption agency." After nine long years, she and Marshall would finally be parents. "The family was so excited. Later that night, Linda woke Marshall to tell him she was having trouble

---

She can't be dead. Don't let her be dead, I silently prayed.

---

breathing," Michael went on, his voice strained. "When Linda got out of bed, she collapsed. Marshall called 911, but... Linda died at the hospital." While my ears were hearing Michael say, "We don't know what happened. Her death is such a mystery. We're waiting for the autopsy report to tell us more," my mind was reliving our youth.

Visions of being in second grade together and watching Linda lug Oscar, her massive cello, back and forth to school; the long, thick braids she wore each day; high school boyfriends; camping; Michael teaching us how to drive; our wedding days; so much time spent together...always together. Then I remembered our last moments together, just six months earlier. We stood in an airport hugging good-bye after a brief "family" reunion when a heavy sense of foreboding washed over me and I started to cry. "I don't want to say good-bye," I told her. "I'm afraid I'll never see you again."

"Of course you'll see me again. And more often, too!" She replied with a light-hearted laugh. But I wasn't as certain as she was. After final hugs, I watched as Linda walked away. That day was bright and sunny but the haunting dread remained heavy inside. Little did I know.

For days after Michael's news, I moved as if in a trance, not fully able to grasp that Linda was gone.

Now, sitting on Matthew's bed, I cradled his small hand into my own, grateful to feel the life in it, grateful for its warmth. "You and Amy are the most important people in the world to me," I struggled. "I love you both more than anybody or anything else, ever. They buried Linda today and I'm so sad about her death, I'm not acting like a very good mom right now," I went on. "I haven't been helping or paying attention to you and Amy like I should and I'm sorry. I want you to know, if I yell at you or cry a lot, it's not because of anything you did. It's just because I'm so sad. After a while the sadness won't feel so strong and I'll be better. I promise."

But Matthew didn't seem to think I owed him an apology. "Mommy," he said with a strong voice, "you don't have to worry about me and Amy. We know Linda was your friend and you loved her, too, but we're not all in the same part so it's OK."

I didn't quite understand. "What do you mean, Bear," I asked, "not in the same part?"

"I mean in your heart. Just because Linda isn't here anymore doesn't make the love go away. You loved her when she lived away from us in New York because it stays in your heart... in a special part... a part just for Linda. That's why hearts have so many chambers."

I couldn't believe my son even understood the word chamber or that he realized the wisdom his message carried. "There's one part for your mom and your dad, and one for friends and different ones for me and Amy. There's one for everybody so it never gets empty. That's how me and Amy know you still love *us*."

I was stunned by his words. *Where did he ever learn that?* No one close had died before, so what experience could have taught him to think that? I scooped Matthew in my arms and whispered, "I didn't know about the special chambers. You are so smart, Bear. So very smart." I pulled the covers snug after prayers, kissed Matthew good-night and pressed a fresh Kleenex against my eyes as I crossed the hall into Amy's room.

Amy had shimmied her little self under her blankets. Her body was so small; she looked more like a doll lying there. Her long, chestnut curls coiled under the pillow's edge where Smokey, a gift from Matthew, lay next to her. I knelt beside Amy's bed offering her the same apology I'd given her brother. "I've been crying a lot, haven't I?" I confessed, stroking her forehead.

"Yes... but it's OK," she reassured me.

"Thank you, sweetie pie," I said. "It's important for people to cry when someone dies, but I want to make sure you know I'm

---

That night, I experienced a true and authentic epiphany.

---

not crying because of anything you or Matthew did. Do you understand that? Do you know what I mean?"

"Yes, Mommy, I know," she answered, "but you don't have to be sad."

"I don't?" I responded, "Why not?"

"Because Linda's really OK," she said, with certainty. "She's happy. She's rocking the babies."

An icy chill prickled up my spine. Amy knew nothing about Linda's desire to be a mother. *What would make her say that?* "She's rocking the babies?" I repeated.

"Yes, Mommy. And you don't have to be sad because Linda's coming back."

A muffled gasp escaped me. I pushed myself away from the bed and stiffly stared into my daughter's soft, blue eyes. My heart was thumping in my ears, as a thousand questions flashed across one second of time. *WHAT did she just say? WHAT is she talking about? Is she suggesting reincarnation? What six year-old knows about that? We've never discussed...How could she.... What IS going on?* "Amy," I cautiously asked, "what do you mean 'Linda's coming back?' How do you know that?"

Abruptly, Amy sat up in bed and propped herself on her elbow to look directly at me. Her serious posture signaled the importance of what she was about to say, and despite her young age, she intuitively knew it. "Because we ALL come back, Mommy," were her exact words. "All of us. I came back, too. And we come back with parts from other people. I have a little bit of Grandpa Frederick and a little bit of...."

My ears went momentarily deaf as Amy continued to list the names of relatives who died before her birth. She never even knew them! What is she saying? WHERE is this coming from? Amy's tone suggested genuine surprise that I did not already know this. She was positively convinced and believed everybody else knew it, too! When she realized this was news to me, she continued, "And Linda's coming back, too. But you won't recognize her right away because she won't look the same. She'll look like somebody else. But you'll know it's her. You'll just *know*."

Amy's eyes remained intent and focused on mine. I was so stunned by this exchange yet at the same time I felt a warm and familiar presence move in. I couldn't think. Thoughts, faces, beliefs,

*I came to believe, more purely, more intensely,
because they understood something I did not.*

truths ricocheted in my mind. *What is happening? Is this real? How did my six year-old daughter come to this wisdom?* I could barely breathe, but it wasn't entirely stemming from shock and disbelief; I wondered if Amy understood a truth I had no knowledge of.

I composed myself well enough to conclude our conversation and tucked my spirited daughter back under the covers with big hugs and good-night prayers. "It makes me feel better to know Linda is rocking the babies, Amy," I whispered. "You know, she always wanted a baby, a little girl, just like you. I'm so glad you told me she's happy."

That night, I experienced a true and authentic epiphany. With every death comes grief and questions; heartbreak so piercing it transcends all space and time. In my despair, my hope became convinced relief would never flower. Yet there, in the midst of my sorrow, my very own children appeared with the power to comfort me. Words. Divinely delivered. And I was moved. I understood. As soon as my faith showed signs of fading, God enlisted two Charges—the faces and voices of those I loved most to bring forth His peace, His understanding and His healing love. He knew I would trust them. I would not question. Within each chamber of the heart, that is how love heals.

I have no rational explanation to offer. But this much is certain: Nothing my blessed family has endured—neither heartache nor financial bankruptcy, not divorce, years of single parenting, family drug addiction, not even death itself, of either Linda or their father later—ever overshadowed the unspoken healing, hope and faith my children infused in me that night.

Amy and Matthew were completely unaware, but because of their rare insight, astonishing wisdom and selfless courage, they held my hand and had an overdue and emotional conversation with me.

From that moment on, every dark stretch along our journey has been illuminated by their light—their trust in what they knew to be true and their childlike faith which surpassed my limited understanding. I came to believe, more purely, more intensely, because they understood something I did not.

As each new day began and each new year passed by, I watched my children grow in age and faith, and by the grace of God, I stood witness as Amy's prophecy came to life. Linda did return. Hers is the laugh, the giggle, the glance, the strength of character and the stillness of voice I now recognize within my lovely daughter, Amy. And in her smile, I am reminded of a favorite photograph and "heart picture"—we're visiting Linda and her family in New York. Matthew is three, and Amy, just one year old. Linda snuggles with my children in her lap, and in remembering that moment every tear we shed, every laugh we shared, every dream we wished for was imprinted on my heart.

This is for you, Lynno. My "adopted sister." My best friend. My spiritual companion. Bless you as you rock the babies.

Dawn-Marie Hanrahan is a celebrated TranSpirational speaker, bestselling author and photographer who travels the world in service to others. Her message of self-empowerment, courage and faith, masterfully combined with her inspiring photography, raises the awareness of her audiences to higher levels of spiritual understanding and personal empowerment. For additional information and updates regarding her next book, Illuminated by Grace – Reality Perfected, please visit www.5StarLifeQuests.com.

Lisa Monaco Gonzales

Sinlessness

It is a typical humid, uncomfortable New England summer night, and though there is some relief from the scorching heat of the day, my sweaty legs still sting when I rip them off the dark leather couch. After a full day frolicking in the pool, I race to the bathroom and cannot remove my bathing suit fast enough. When I step into my snow-white nightgown with its elegant scoop neck and fluffy, puffy short sleeves, I am a princess. No one is prettier than me, not even Cinderella!

With not a care in the world, I am elated to be at my friend Marlene's house for a sleepover. "Let's be cheerleaders," she suggests to Lauren, her younger sister, and me.

We shout, "Go Team!" and jump up and down. We peek around the corner into the dark den, where the only light in the room comes from the television. Their mom has disappeared, but their dad, our trusted adult friend, is waiting for our brilliant performance. He is sprawled out on his big black leather couch with his big round body tightly squeezed into his worn-out robe. His furry beard is quite beastly, and yet he is as jolly as old Saint Nick.

Marlene asks her dad to set the stage by asking, "Who should we be?"

He replies in his deep, gentle voice, "My three princesses, so beautiful with grace, please enter the king's ballroom, where I will introduce you to the prince, my son, who is looking for his forever after."

We leap into the room, waving and giggling at the king. As he waves back, he gazes into our eyes and says, "I am mesmerized by your beauty, my three princesses. Keep dancing until it is time to meet the prince." Marlene and Lauren vie for their dad's attention, but he chooses me. He pats the remaining small space on the couch to show me where to sit, right next to the king. *What a thrill! Did I win? Is the prince going to marry me?* I wonder, with great anticipation: *What comes next?*

I feel him place his heavy ape arm around my little shoulders. My neck itches from his coarse hair. My muscles tighten when he begins massaging my neck. I am confused. Something doesn't feel

---

*No one is prettier than me,
not even Cinderella!*

---

right. *Is this part of the game? Is this how the king picks out the princess for the prince?* I don't know the answers, but I do know I'm not interested in playing this game anymore.

The sisters are still dancing around us, oblivious to our interactions, and I wish one of them would just take my place. Maybe they like this game, but I don't. How do I tell everyone I'm finished and I just want to go and hang out with Marlene? Her dad may get angry and tell my parents that I didn't play well with the girls and cannot come over again. I could be punished.

He lifts me and places me on his lap; it feels like a shaggy rug. I feel dizzy. My stomach drops. *Am I sick? Do I need to go to the hospital? What is he doing?* His hairy gorilla hand suddenly drops deep into the front of my top as he continues to pet me like a cat. *Help! Someone make him stop!* My mouth is dry and my voice has drifted far, far, away. I am trembling and my vision is blurry. My chest feels so heavy; is he standing on it? The butterflies in my stomach flutter out of control. I cannot think. *Let me out. Am I going crazy? Am I dying?*

I feel a tap on my shoulder, "Are you ready to play Monopoly upstairs in my bedroom?" Marlene inquires.

"Let's go!" I reply and I am released. My legs are wobbly, but I make them run.

I'm hiding out in Marlene's room playing Monopoly, distracting myself from my reality until morning, when I can finally escape. Just as the threat of her father is drifting away, the door to her room cracks open. There he is, half-naked in his deteriorated robe, with a devious smile. Like a snake in his familiar habitat, hunting down his prey, he slithers over to the bed where his daughter and I are playing Monopoly and coils up close behind me. A cold sweat drenches my body from head to toe. He leans closer to my body. Suddenly, I feel a push under my bottom and a hairy sensation as his grotesque gorilla hand slips inside my panties.

Vomit erupts from my esophagus into my throat. I force it back. The room spins and my thoughts race. *I'm losing the game; it will be his fault if I lose the game. I cannot concentrate. I must gain control and win the game!* My guts are inside out as I roll the dice and end up in JAIL. Marlene lands on Reading Railroad. "Let's negotiate," she says.

"Let's not," is all I can reply.

Impending doom blinds my vision as her dad steals my sinlessness from my dainty little soul. I'm stuttering and knocking down houses and hotels like a tornado. "What is wrong with you?" she asks.

How could she not know? Maybe she knows, but would rather it be me than her tonight? I get a double and am out of JAIL. The snake slithers away. The storm is over, but darkness remains. The game continues until the sun peeks through the blinds. The game finally winds down and we agree to end the all-nighter without a winner. The doorbell rings and off I go. I feel icky inside, broken, scared. As I run to the car I know deep in my gut that this will be a secret I will never share. Sitting in the back seat, my head hangs low. *Was this my fault? Why did I let him? Please don't make me go back.*

But I did go back. My parents took me to many other parties at Marlene's house. I wondered: *Can't you see that I hate this place? Please figure it out. I don't play with the kids; I stay right by your side during the whole party.* But when Mom asked, "Why don't you play with your friend anymore?" I replied, "We had a fight." How could I tell her what Marlene's father, *my mother's friend,* does to me? She might not believe me. She might get mad. She might stop loving me. And in time the memories were buried, where they could not hurt or shame me any more.

And in time the memories were buried, where they could not hurt or shame me any more.

Now, in my early twenties, I am a college graduate, living in another state, and employed at my first "real" job. It's a dreary day; I decide to watch a movie. The weather reflects my mood as I wallow in my loneliness. The movie on the television is intense; my insides speak to me as my brain stays busy processing the plot. My chest is tightening. Tears pour from my eyes like a rainstorm as anxiety overwhelms me. I try to stand up, but my balance is off and I drop to the floor. I am hysterical, full of fear, but what am I afraid of? *Am I sick? Do I need to go to the hospital? Am I going to die, here on the floor, all by myself?* Curled in fetal position, I grasp my gut, begging for relief from the pain. Memories flood my mind. "Stop it, stop touching me," I cry out loud.

Once the repressed memories reappeared, I deep-dove into therapy and support groups. Telling that long-buried dark secret to my parents was a huge risk, but part of the healing process. Mom's reception of this devastating news transformed into an investigation and I knew she was on my side. I slept a bit better that night. Later, Mom learned he had accosted many girls.

Another twenty years pass, and I am with my aunt at a launch party for a book in which her friend has written a chapter. People are signing books, cameras flash. We grab a bite to eat and find a place for ourselves in the back, to people-watch and chat. A fragile-looking woman, Julie Thong, stands as tall as she can to reach the microphone and begins reading her chapter, *The Smell of Grass.* As I listen to her story of how her family was violated and the devastating experiences she survived in the killing fields of Cambodia, my lips quiver and the tears stream down my face. My stomach is in knots and I am afraid I may throw up.

Don't listen to her, get out, run! I am bent over, holding in my guts as I try to push my emotions back inside. My aunt pats my back and whispers, "Are you okay? Maybe we should leave." Composing myself the best I can, I convince her we can stay. As the story becomes darker, my thoughts deteriorate into helplessness and I realize that once again, the little girl in me is reliving the incident.

*And finally, I know in my heart I can
no longer keep this story to myself.*

On the ride home, I apologize to my aunt. "I am perplexed about my reaction to that woman's story." As we discuss her story, I clench my fists, my stomach muscles tighten and my neck is stiff. *What is wrong with me?* Something inside me screams to get out. *What if I open up and share my deep dark secret? Will she still love me? Will she judge me? Will she believe me?* My voice begins crawling up from my diaphragm, closer and closer to my vocal chords. As I share my story with her, the demons are freed and the pressure releases.

And finally, I know in my heart I can no longer keep this story to myself. "My children and the children of the world need protection," I say out loud.

My deep dark secret must be released; my story must be told to preserve the sinlessness of our children. The time has come to use my voice, the one I never could as a child. I was one out of three girls molested by their eighteenth birthday; for boys that statistic is one out of every seven. These numbers reflect what we know. There are plenty of incidences that are not reported and that is why, for the pedophile, it is the perfect crime. Most child predators are among our circle of family, friends and community; ninety percent of molestations are perpetrated by people we know.

My work is to educate parents and guardians; with knowledge comes power. And for my fellow survivors, who understand this pain, I hope to inspire them to transcend the despair.

I share this story for all of the princes and princesses, the superheroes and rock stars, the ninjas and fairies, the wizards and ballerinas, the cowboys and mermaids. For all of the innocent children. Every single one.

Lisa Monaco Gonzales is an author and advocate of child safety. Lisa graduated from Bryant College in Rhode Island with a BS in business. Her corporate background is in sales, marketing, and training. As a survivor of sexual abuse, she learned early to push through obstacles with persistence and resilience. Through her speaking, Lisa brings resources and tools to help adults guard children against sexual predators. Through her children's books, she empowers our adults of the future to speak out. Born and raised in Connecticut, Lisa now resides in sunny San Diego, California, with her loving husband and two beautiful children. Connect with Lisa at www. LisaMonacoGonzales.com.

Corinna Rogers

I Choose to Thrive!

I t's dark when I arrive at the pharmacy. The peaceful, pre-dawn stillness matches my own still-sleepy, relaxed mood. *Someday I'll have a corporate career in a plush office.* But for now, I start my opening duties as manager, finishing them easily and efficiently I'm here first—and alone—to receive the usual early morning delivery. When I hear plastic crates being moved around outside, then the bell, it's just the normal routine. The delivery dock's door has no peephole, but I'm expecting the stock employee, and I open the door to let him in.

A gun points straight into my face. Behind it stands a short, stocky man wearing a black ski mask. I hear a long, long scream; I don't realize it is coming from me. "Shut up, bitch!" The man yells, but I can't stop. I can't think, can't run, can't fight—only scream. "Move, move!" he shouts and shoves me into the manager's office, pushing my face up against the safe.

"Open it!" Hands shaking, I spin the dial, but I can't read the numbers. *This is insane—I've worked this combination a million times!* There is nothing but me, the dial and my failure to open the safe. In a rage, he shoves the gun's cold barrel into the back of my head, shouting, "Open it bitch, or you are going to die! Open it or I will shoot your ass! Do you want to die?! Open it! NOW!" The shouting goes on forever. *This is it. This is how I am going to die.*

Finally, the safe opens! He shoves me aside, grabs money from the top couple of trays, then turns back, staring, calculating. *He thinks I know who he is. Why?* Everything is covered but his eyes. Still, he pushes me down on my knees, rams a plastic grocery bag into my hands and yells, "Put it on your head!" Something inside me snaps. There is NO WAY I am going to let him put that bag over my head! This is the one thing I cannot do if I am going to survive.

Without thinking, I jerk back. *I have to get away!* Startled, he leaps up and runs out the door. I stagger to my feet, slam the office

---

This is it. This is how I am going to die.

---

door, lock myself in. *Call 911!* I shake violently. A series of beeps tells me I'm being patched through. "I manage this store. I've just been robbed."

"Is the robber still there? Are you in immediate danger?" *If he was still here, I'd already be dead.* I stand in the office shaking, listening for any small sounds outside. The stillness is eerie, scary, not peaceful.

When the police arrive, I call my manager and have her come and take over the store. Somehow, I get home—maybe I drive, maybe someone drives me. The company requires me to go through a post-incident process, a sort of "Kum Ba Ya," let's-get-you-back-to-work measure. But I know I won't go back. I'm out the door.

Two weeks later, I am home alone. It is after midnight, and I have just gone to bed. I've locked my bedroom door beforehand (a habit born of growing up in a large family) and am just dozing off when I hear a loud crash. *Someone is breaking in! How could this happen to me AGAIN? I live a mainstream lifestyle! I live in a nice condo, in a good neighborhood—I live on the second floor, for goodness sake!* I jump out of bed, reach for my phone and dive into my bathroom in one fluid motion. I hear another loud bang as the exterior door of my condo comes crashing in. *Answer, Answer!*

The 911 operator finally picks up. "The police are already in your complex. They are in pursuit. This perpetrator is already wounded from a shoot-out with the police. They will catch him. What can you hear?" the dispatcher asks.

"I hear sounds but I can't tell," I whisper urgently. *This guy knows I'm in the house.*

"Don't go out," I am told. *As if I would!* I am practically glued to the door. The 911 operator is still talking, but all I hear is the sound of someone rummaging around my condo, banging in and out of cabinets and closets.

Then I hear police radios squeaking on the other side of the door. "Ma'am, this is the police. We've got him," a voice says. "You're safe. You can come out now." I hear the radios, I know the police are real, but it doesn't matter. I cannot open that door. I have been here before, and if I am to survive, I cannot open that door.

I can't answer their questions intelligibly. Words are locked inside. *They must think I'm crazy. How can I explain to them that I just can't come out?* My sister, who lives in the same complex, arrives after I am finally able to answer one of their questions: "Is there anyone we can call?" I don't remember actually coming out of the bathroom or into the living room. There is a swarm of

---

I have been here before, and if I am to survive, I cannot open that door.

---

cops—ten or fifteen of them in that small room. It's like someone else's house, someone's house in a horror movie. The doorframe hangs out of the wall, and blood is smeared across the table and down the hall from the intruder's gunshot wound. He had been naked, I'm told, and was probably searching for something to wear and maybe reduce the flow of blood.

I don't go back to that condo until moving day. I never miss a beat. I put on a suit and go to my new job at the corporate office every day. *I am always the strong one.* I never tell anyone about my experiences. But one afternoon, I go downstairs to drop off a package at the shipping office, and when the elevator door opens, there is a man standing right in the doorway. No doubt he is headed up to his own office, but seeing him freaks me out so badly I have to go sit in my car for thirty minutes, shaking uncontrollably in an unstoppable flood of terror.

I feel fractured and raw. I am like an egg that has cracked in the boiling process. My emotions ooze from the cracks, and there is nothing I can do to get them back inside and under my control. I walk a tightrope, trying to maintain balance, but anything can throw me off-kilter. I swing wildly between being irritable and angry to feeling completely disconnected from the things and

---

*In the course of an hour, I learned that
I had a textbook case of Post-Traumatic
Stress Disorder. This changed everything!*

---

people I used to love. At family events, I sit outside the circle of light and laughter and think, *What's the point?* Worst are the moments of terror. At any moment some benign event or peripheral shadow can hurtle me back into a maelstrom of fear and panic. *I am going insane*, I think. *I will not recover from this.*

A constant rush of adrenaline pumps through my veins, and I have a heightened awareness—like a super-hero "spidey sense," except there is nothing cool about it. Continual threat analyses play through my mind; I can tell you in great detail who is around me, what they are doing and what they have done in the last ten minutes. Before I can accept any invitation, I must work out a whole list of potential scenarios and troubleshoot each one. I say "Yes" only if I can ensure I will be safe, if I can eliminate the possibility of finding terror waiting for me somewhere in the activity.

Several months after the break-in, my mom, sister and best friends intervened. They hugged me, saying gently, "You need professional help." Here I was with a bachelor's degree in psychology, generally optimistic about the value of counseling when appropriate, but for some reason I was totally resistant to therapy. *I don't need it. I'm strong enough to get through this on my own.* But my loved ones stood firm.

The very first session changed everything. My therapist, a soft-spoken, kind woman, laid a piece of paper in front of me and said, "Take a look at this list and tell me what describes your feelings."

I scanned the thirty items. I said, "I've had everything on this list! This is my life right now." "I want you to know," she said, looking at me levelly, "that this list is the criteria for defining Post-Traumatic Stress Disorder." *You tricked me,* I thought; but she had used the right tactic. If she had come out and said, "I think you have PTSD," I would have blown it off.

In the course of an hour, I learned that I had a textbook case of Post-Traumatic Stress Disorder. This changed everything! I was shocked. I had never even considered it. I thought PTSD was something only combat soldiers had. But I had almost all of the diagnostic indicators: irritability, anger, poor concentration, a startle reaction, difficulty remembering, hyper-vigilance and avoidance. I was not only avoiding any discussion of the experiences, but everything that reminded me of them as well. I had moved to a new home in a new part of town, split from my roommate, changed jobs and cut all my old night-owl activities out of my life completely.

I'm not losing my mind! I hated the thought of being labeled a victim or, worse, insane. But having PTSD meant my responses were merely reactions to extraordinary stress, not some kind of personal weakness. It all fit inside that context—what a relief! My feelings suddenly became logical; they made sense! That first week I started doing some of the things my therapist asked me to do, though I thought it odd that my treatment included seeing happy comedies and watching cartoons. It was like I was my own little science project. After about a month, I realized that the spidey sense was almost gone. *I can breathe again!*

And then my breath was sucked away again. Waking alone one night in my new, safe apartment, I spotted someone's head moving in the dark of the kitchen. *Oh my God! What have I done to deserve this? I can't go through this again!* Nauseated with fear, too paralyzed to move, I waited for the intruder to come into my bedroom. He didn't; just kept moving back and forth. For five unbearable minutes, his pattern never varied. *Could it be a shadow? Should I call the police or not? Am I overreacting?*

I grabbed the phone and called a friend, who persuaded me to turn on a light. I think I could have lifted a car more easily than I turned on that light. But I did it... and saw the balloon a co-worker had given me earlier that day bobbing lazily in the kitchen. I sobbed in relief, then in anger and grief—how long would I live with this fear, these reactions?

But over time, I found I was developing the tools to prevent these flare-ups of panic. I learned to check myself: *Are you responding to something in the past? Are you making a choice in this moment?* Practice was critical, as with all new skills. It was easy to react swiftly in terror and much harder to slowly evaluate the reality of risk. But as I learned to do it, I learned I really *was* strong—strong enough to know when to seek help, when to lean on friends, when to learn new skills and when to stand alone.

If I had been told what was to come, that year of the crime spree, I never would have believed it—and I never would have believed I could survive it all. But I did—and what a blessing it has been. I now know that it's really okay if I'm not in control of everything and that I can accept help. I was so independent before, I had no idea how essential my loved ones really are, or how important it is for people to lean on each other. Knowing it is sometimes just as generous to receive as to give—I wouldn't trade that for anything.

Terrible things will happen. An infinite number of unforeseen events might derail us. But none of us are meant to live in isolation or fear. We have the power to see beyond the scary pictures superimposed over our lives and reclaim the lives *we choose*. It has been fifteen years now. And I did more than survive, I thrived!

Corinna Rogers, the voice for women's accelerated professional success, is a transformational author, speaker and mentor. During her years consulting in the IT industry, Corinna was often the only woman at the executive table. This experience fueled her desire to help young women advance more rapidly in their chosen professions. Her experiences taught her that women need more focused professional skills and development. She transforms girls preparing to enter their careers and women professionals seeking to accelerate their success. Corinna recently co-authored a book with Sheri McConnell, CEO of Smart Women's Institute: Smart Women Live Their Why. Connect with Corinna at www.SheVelocity.com.

Meade W. Malone

A Walk of Faith

A s I opened the gate of the Anegada Methodist Church and
readied myself to walk the path that led to the front door,
I fought desperately to calm my fears and subdue my troubled
thoughts. Over and over again, the events of Friday replayed
themselves in my mind, crowding out the sermon God had laid
on my heart for the congregation this Sunday and threatening any
hope I had of preaching effectively. The thoughts felt like a prison,
and the battle to release my mind was intense.

I am a businessman as well as a preacher, and the firm I had
purchased the previous year in the summer of 1998, from the
largest professional services firm in the world, was now on its own
and lacking the built-in protections and hundreds of partners
its parent firm had provided. During this transitional period,
balancing costs and the uncertainty of clients paying us on time,
we had hit a difficult point financially. And months ago, I had made
a decision in faith that now brought a lot of what-ifs along with it.

*What if I still don't have the money to pay the staff on Tuesday?
What if the credibility of the firm is damaged? What if we have to
close it down? What if we get negative press and can't recover? What
if I fail? What if I don't pass the test of faith?*

But then, as I walked up the stairs and into the empty church,
I was struck by an awesome presence. I felt the Holy Spirit there,

a great calming, reassuring presence, like someone I had been searching for whom I knew could help me but had been unable to find until that moment. My anxious fears subsided in a flood of relief. He *was* there—I was not alone, He would see me through. In my spirit I heard a rattling, as the chains that had bound me fell to the ground and my prison door opened. *Truly,* I cried, *where the Spirit of the Lord is, there is liberty!* I raised my hands in the empty church and simply worshipped all by myself.

Back on Friday afternoon, sitting in the conference room at work, I'd heard a knock on the door and invited Julia, the accountant, to enter. As she approached me, the atmosphere in the room changed

---

The thoughts felt like a prison, and the battle to release my mind was intense.

---

immediately—the look of concern on her face told a story all by itself. She sat down with the bank folder in her hand and said, very softly, "Mr. Malone? You know that Tuesday is payday."

"Yes," I replied, waiting for her to continue.

Then, just as softly, she said, "We don't have enough money to pay the staff."

Immediately fear gripped me, and the cold conference room suddenly became too warm. Beads of sweat formed on my forehead. At first I resisted with all my might, but after weighing all the options I believed I had no other choice but to call my bank manager and ask him to extend a line of credit for the firm.

This news felt like another great test of my faith. Only a few months ago, just before leaving for New York on a business trip, I had stopped in my office to look at the bank folder and realized that the bank balances were very low. But I was comforted by the fact that I had savings that could be used as collateral.

On the flight to New York, however, the Holy Spirit had spoken to me and had told me that I should give away all of our savings. My question was, "All?" and the response was, "Give it all away!" As I sat in silence on the plane, I grappled with this guidance.

"God, is this really real?" His soft, still voice reminded me, "I am the One who has made it possible for you to purchase the firm. You must rely on Me to provide for it."

"Yes, Lord, I will do as You instruct," I whispered, and a sense of calm and peace swept over me.

On landing in New York I immediately called my wife, Sandra. When I told her what had happened, her quick response was, "If the Lord said that is what we must do, then we should do it." A great sense of relief flooded over me that we had agreed to follow the Lord's instruction. I later shared with my parents and siblings what the Lord had said, and they too agreed that I should be obedient. And so I had said *yes* to the Holy Spirit's bidding to give all of our savings to a cause close to our hearts. That meant that when this news had come on Friday, I no longer had collateral to use for the firm.

Now, in the empty church, the Holy Spirit spoke to me again and said that I should cancel the new line of credit I was planning to use to pay the staff, following the same process I had used to establish it. It was as if the prison doors were closing again.

"Is it really you speaking, Lord?" I asked. "Must I take it away? How can I know for sure that it's you speaking?"

The answer came: "Read John 13:1-20. I am going to make the way for you to wash the feet of the congregation. Get up and go to the other side of the church—there you will find a bucket and a clean rag you will use to dry the feet you wash. When you have done these things that I have told you, then you will know that I have spoken to you."

I felt an incredible peace. My prison door reopened and, once more, my chains were gone. I went over and opened a door on the other side of the church—there was the bucket, and there was the rag!

I looked up to heaven and worshipped the Lord. I still felt some apprehension, though, about how the congregation would respond to the invitation for me to wash their feet. (After all, I had never heard of Methodists doing such a thing!) But I went ahead and filled the bucket with water and hid it and the rag under a chair while I waited for the congregation to gather.

Our church is very small, and twelve people came that day. At the end of the sermon I issued the invitation. To my utter amazement, the congregation (all except for two ladies wearing pantyhose they could not comfortably remove) came forward to the altar, one by one, in silence. They sat down, removed their shoes and socks and

---

I felt an incredible peace. My prison door reopened and, once more, my chains were gone.

---

rolled up their pants legs for me to wash and dry their feet, just as the Lord had said. Then we all moved to the front of the altar, where I anointed them with oil and prayed over them. When we finished, the congregation returned to their seats, still holding that reverent silence.

It was extraordinary. I was awed, amazed by the power of the Holy Spirit to create this atmosphere in which every man and woman loosed their inhibitions and the norms of the church to come together in this silent, reverent place. And I felt honored and privileged to witness and be a part of it. By the time the service ended, my doubts and fears had been replaced by deep joy and confidence that God would provide all that was needed to pay the bills—just as He had promised.

When I arrived at work the next morning, I called Julia into the conference room and told her all that had happened. She was very worried, but she was also a pastor's daughter and understood the concept of having one's faith tested. So she nodded quietly when I gave her instructions to draft a letter to the bank canceling my request for credit.

All that day the bank manager kept calling to speak with me, but I refused his calls. I was determined to shut the door on any challenges to my faith and to allow nothing to distract me from the path I had been instructed to walk.

Later in the day, Julia came to ask me what to do about payroll, which was due the next day, Tuesday. "Write the checks and give them to the staff," I told her, smiling.

I could see the despair on her face, but she forced it into a nervous smile. "But Mr. Malone, there isn't enough money in the bank. If they go to cash their checks, we will be embarrassed."

Once again I said to her, "Write the checks and give them to the staff—I believe that God will provide, just as He promised." Instantly, her expression changed. Despair was replaced by quiet faith, and she agreed to follow my instructions.

As I went to bed that night, the what-ifs came back in a flood and threatened to overwhelm me. I twisted and turned all night, fighting with all my might to hold my ground. About four o'clock Tuesday morning, as I lay on the bed, engulfed in fear, these words

---

*I was determined to shut the door
on any challenges to my faith and to
allow nothing to distract me from the
path I had been instructed to walk.*

---

came to me: "Meade, you will not be put to shame; I have made your portion sure." I began to shout for joy and fell on my knees as I thanked and worshipped God.

Later that morning, there was a knock on the conference room door, and Julia entered, smiling ecstatically. "Boss," she said, eyes shining, "God has come through for us. I just checked the bank. Fifty thousand dollars was credited to our account this morning! We have more than enough to pay the staff and our bills!"

I sprang from my chair as "Hallelujah!" burst from my lips.

This is a deliverance story; I firmly believe that the Lord was prompting me, setting me up so that He could do according to His Word and deliver me in times of trouble. And it reaffirmed for me that I serve a God who can be trusted, who is faithful to His Word. Ever since that Tuesday, I worry less. Instead, I trust that God will be with me as I walk forward in faith.

Meade W. Malone is Managing Director of MWM Global Holdings Group Limited, which provides insolvency, financial restructuring, audit, pension and corporate and trust services. A former Partner in Charge at PricewaterhouseCoopers British Virgin Islands, he graduated magna cum laude from Pace University, where he also earned his MBA. He has held the positions of Deputy Financial Secretary in the Ministry of Finance and Acting Permanent Secretary in the Chief Minister's Office for the Government of the Virgin Islands. Meade is a Local Preacher on Trial in the Methodist Church, the leader of the Fort Hill prayer group and the author of The Plan – Unlocking God's Financial Blessing for Your Life. *Connect with Meade at www.MeadeMalone.com.*

Angelife Pardo

Coming Alive

I awoke on what seemed to be a normal Wednesday morning but was in fact only the first in a series of days and events that would turn my five-year-old world upside down. "When is Daddy going to be home from work?" I anxiously asked my mother after dinner.

"He's not here anymore, baby. He's on an airplane to America," she responded sadly.

Currently, seven million Filipinos working in Australia, Europe, Asia and North America financially support thirty-five million family members struggling to survive in the impoverished economy of the Philippines. To a five year-old, however, the loss of her father was more difficult to understand. "He kissed you goodbye this morning while you were sleeping," my mother said, a tear rolling down her cheek.

Confused and unsatisfied with her response, I went to bed unsettled and decided with a heart full of hope that I would wake up one morning and have my dad back again. Mornings and nights passed only to have hope run empty and disappointment fill me back to full. A five year-old's vocabulary was not mature enough to describe this feeling of deep sadness, but even at that age I could not deny its presence. It was like a new stepfather, there in place of my father's loving spirit.

A few months later, it was my mother's turn to go. I remember standing on the porch and waving goodbye to her as she hurried away to catch her flight. One of my aunts explained that she would be leaving to join my dad. I didn't know how to react. I went upstairs to an empty room and cried alone on my bed. I was so confused. *Why are my parents leaving me behind? Do they not want me anymore?* Innately, I felt I would never see them again. I was six years old. I didn't know how to verbalize my feelings. I didn't know how to ask for help—all I knew was that I had a gaping hole in my chest and nothing to fill it with.

Everything looked so dark. After crying myself to sleep every night for weeks, I accepted that my parents weren't coming back. If they didn't want me, then I didn't need them either. My grandparents were my caretakers now, but what if they left too? I tried to find a sense of safety and assurance, the kind that only the presence of my parents could give me—but there was only emptiness accompanied by a deep sense of loss. I knew that I had

---

Innately, I felt I would never see them again.

---

to find a way to be strong to protect my brother Angelo. He was only four and couldn't fall asleep unless he held my hand in both of his. It was just me and him now.

Angelo and I shared a room, with two little beds, upstairs in our grandparents' house, while all the other relatives slept downstairs. One day I was awakened from my nap when I felt someone lie down behind me. I snuck a peek at my brother's bed: he had his back turned and was sound asleep, so I knew it wasn't him; it was a grown-up, one of my relatives. I didn't know why he was there, touching me, but it didn't feel right. Hoping that he would just go away, I pretended that I was still asleep, but he continued to touch me. He took off my shorts slowly and then my underwear.

I didn't want to scream because I didn't want to frighten Angelo. I started to cry but kept as quiet as I could. "What are you doing?" I pleaded.

"This is a game," the man whispered. "This is fun for you. You have to keep it a secret. You can't tell anyone because you will get a spanking for being a bad girl." Fear engulfed me, along with confusion and the emptiness of not feeling the safe presence of my mother and father. Obedience, I reasoned, was the only way to save myself; so silence became my comrade. Only years later did I realize that I had bargained my voice, my right to speak and be heard, for the price of safety.

Our door didn't have a doorknob, so my grandma could just look through the hole and check on us. He would stuff it with a blanket when he came to "play with me," and when I saw that, I knew what was about to happen. I wasn't thinking of whether this

I had bargained my voice, my right to speak and be heard, for the price of safety.

"game" was right or wrong. I just didn't want to be a bad girl and give my grandparents a reason not to want me either. Wasn't that why my parents left me? I also didn't want my brother to become involved in this game. *Don't let him wake up. He can't see this. If he sees, can I protect him?* I thought, *If he's doing it to me, then he won't do it to him.* I felt powerless and alone.

Numbing and distracting myself gradually became amnesia. I don't know how long these games lasted, but I started to feel less of my body and retreated to safe places in my mind. After two years, it was finally our turn to leave for America. When I was reunited with my parents I didn't know how to feel. Fear, confusion and sadness had filled the areas of my heart where love and adoration for them once resided. They were strangers to me, just as my secret experiences were to them.

It wasn't until I was attending my new elementary school that we were taught about sexual harassment and good touch and bad touch. I reasoned that if abuse is a bad thing, then I must have been a bad girl and deserved it. I wanted to pretend that it never happened because when the seed of guilt takes root, the roots of fear are even deeper. To admit that I had been abused, I felt I had to kill a part of myself to pull it out and expose it. *SO WHAT if it happened to me? I survived. When people look at me, it's not like they can see it. How could it hurt me to not say anything? I have more to lose by telling the truth.*

What does it feel like to not be seen? What does it feel like not to really live and be *alive?* On the surface I was happy and put together, but fear, guilt, shame and judgment lingered in the background of every experience and negated every victory. Part of me wanted to stay in the dark and shrink back, but another part of me yearned for acknowledgment.

As I grew older, I experienced that duality in painful ways. Once I was in a relationship, I would sabotage it. *Do I really deserve this attention? Do I really deserve this person?* I saw their worth, but not my own. I felt responsible for everyone but me and believed that I did not deserve help and support from myself, for myself.

I thought, *I am not good enough* and believed this lie for twenty-two years. But in 2010, everything changed. I had an uncomfortable exchange with an elderly man in the ministry, a person well respected for his gifts. He was visiting the city and after he requested that I bring him something to eat, he asked to speak with me privately, to thank me for my hospitality I presumed. Our conversation started amiably and after sharing stories from traveling the world, he proceeded to tell me about the presidents and numerous people of notoriety that he was personable with and whom he knew could open doors of opportunity for me.

Suddenly his voice lowered as he inched closer, *I can take you with me to travel the world and meet them. Your father doesn't have to know, okay?* He caressed my arm and looked at me intensely. I could not speak. I stopped breathing as my entire body stiffened— like prey spotted by a predator. But despite the paralysis, I realized what was happening and knew immediately what I had to do.

In my childhood, I thought maybe I was wrong about the abuse, that it was my fault, that I caused it to happen and that no one would believe me if I spoke the truth. But I wasn't a child anymore.

At 27 years old I knew that it was no one else's responsibility but mine to protect myself. I hesitated and feared that I would not be supported or believed, but I had no doubt that only the truth could set me free—from this situation and everything I had tolerated in my past up until that point. Still, thoughts raged—*What if they don't believe me? What if they say that it was my fault?*

Amidst the chatter, I heard a still voice clearly say, "*Courage is not the absence of fear, but rather the judgment that something else is more important than fear*" (Ambrose Redmoon). At that moment I knew that my freedom and my life—*my truth*—was

---

*None of those fears can co-exist
when I'm truly alive and creating.*

---

more important than the fear that haunted me for so long. I immediately reached out to a trusted friend who knew whom to call that could handle the situation appropriately. After a series of phone calls from other leaders in the ministry to whom I recounted my experience, I was assured that I was safe. The gentleman was questioned, reprimanded and asked to leave.

After being seen, being believed and being supported, I saw me, the *real* me. And suddenly, I felt more of the world. I felt sensations in my hands, as if they barely existed before. It was very surreal. I could see and hear more clearly and feel more of life in me and around me. It dawned on me how much power I had in using my voice, and I felt the freedom in being seen and heard. Outside of my shell and in the light, I suddenly came alive.

That experience helped me to recognize that I had the power to choose and take action. I now understand choice as a facet of self-expression, so when I can create, I express the authentic me that I know is worthy, valuable, capable, adequate and powerful. I started to see and become the real me—the creator I was born to be rather than the victim I learned to be. Victims believe they don't have the right to choose who they are and what happens to them. Their very being is always under the threat of fear, resulting in beliefs of inadequacy and confusion over their true power and capacity. I was no longer that woman.

After facing my fears and experiencing the power of using my voice, I wanted to know more about my true potential. George Bernard Shaw said, "Life isn't about finding yourself. Life is about creating yourself." What else was I capable of being and creating? With childlike faith, I now run to challenges, face my fears and express myself without worrying about what others will think. None of those fears can co-exist when I'm truly alive and creating.

The first great thing I chose to create was a connection with my parents by choosing to be honest about my past experiences instead of worrying about how they would react. *I can't make that fear my driving force—that mindset is over.* Instead, I focused on expressing myself by telling my parents about the molestation. I went to them not as a victim but as an empowered woman who chooses to let my experiences strengthen me. Now both of them see me in a different light: instead of seeing the child they had abandoned and felt perpetually guilty about, they finally saw me as me, the unbreakable woman who came alive once again.

Angelife is an avid entrepreneur, adventurer, dancer, and runner extraordinaire, always searching to accomplish new feats in business and self-discovery. Constantly brimming with joy and positive energy, one tends to wonder if her happy juices are legal. She enjoys life by finding creative ways to express freedom, love, hope, balance and connection in the world. Connect with Angelife at www.AngelifePardo.com.

Linda J. Davis

The Least of These

L ying in my hospital bed, staring alternately at the ceiling and four sterile white walls, I was consumed with loneliness and worry. My body had betrayed me at the most inconvenient time. *Why do I have to be here NOW?* I asked myself. *If this had to happen, why could it not have waited until I finished the proposal for this million-dollar staffing contract?* I don't have the time for this. There is too much riding on me.

Recently, my health had begun to deteriorate. On some days, I could barely pull myself out of bed because of the fatigue. On other days, I was too weak to even talk on the phone. I had consulted one doctor after another, most of whom attributed my symptoms to "women's issues."

After spending countless hours with general practitioners, a gynecologist, two internal medicine specialists and gastro-enterologists, and after submitting to dozens of procedures and tests, I had not gotten better, and my fatigue grew worse. I was admitted to the hospital for testing and observation, and for the last two days I had been prodded, poked, stuck and x-rayed in almost every part of my exhausted body.

How did I get here? After all, my entire life I've worked hard to be the best, to do the best. In my mind, that was the only way to prove myself worthy of being loved.

Growing up, I figured that if I worked hard enough, I would prove without any reservations that I was worthy of my mother's love and acceptance. I cared for my five brothers and sisters the few times my mother worked outside the home, and to keep the house sparkling when she was away, I cleaned like a hyper-caffeinated maid. I wanted so badly to meet her high standards! I swept and mopped the floors, took out the trash, made the beds, scoured the bathrooms and put everything in its proper place. I inspected every crack and corner to see if I'd missed anything. I even pulled the heavy sofa-bed from the wall and mopped behind it.

I wanted to surprise Mother—to make her proud of me. I idolized her. Despite her limited schooling, she and Dad raised nine kids and made sure we got a good education. We were the first family on the block to get a brand new set of Collier's Encyclopedias, bought with money that could have gone for clothes, shoes or utility bills.

Though the neighbors marveled at how clean our house was, considering how many children lived there, my efforts never passed the "white glove" test. I may have cleaned behind the sofa-bed, but I'd forgotten to haul the heavy refrigerator into the middle of the kitchen to mop behind it. As usual, I'd let my mother down. I listened quietly while she recited my shortcomings before trudging to my bedroom. Each one felt like a bullet, piercing my innermost being. Behind my closed door, I cried like an abandoned baby. *What can I do to be worthy of her love?* Why did I keep failing? Nothing I did was ever good enough for my mother, which meant I wasn't good enough. All I could do was promise myself that, next time, I would do better. I would work harder to earn her love.

By age thirty-four, I'd left these childish insecurities behind me… or so I thought. I was Manager of Credit Administration for Toronto Dominion Bank, overseeing the legal documentation of loans in a three billion-dollar portfolio. I was earning more money than ever, despite the embarrassment of not finishing college. This shortcoming tugged at my conscience like a pouty child at the hem of my dress, but I knew I'd cross this task off my "to do" list— someday.

On my third year into the job, management decided to move the bank to Houston, Texas. I was married at the time and had no desire to relocate. On the other hand, I knew that obtaining a similar position would be difficult without a college degree. I had some thinking to do. After mulling things over, I said to myself, "When God closes a door, He opens a window. This might be the shove I need to start my own business!"

In August 1990, with heart in hand, my entire savings and a loan of forty-thousand dollars, I opened the doors of Dynamic People. Within two years I opened the second office, and within three years, I had transformed my franchise into one of the most successful in company history, posting annual revenues of three million dollars. Awards and accolades poured in. Perched seventeen stories above Peachtree Street, I had achieved my dream

---

Why did I keep failing? Nothing I did
was ever good enough for my mother,
which meant I wasn't good enough.

---

of becoming a business owner by helping others to realize theirs. At my Dynamic People temporary-help franchises, the staff and I worked to supply training and find jobs for people of all ages, incomes and backgrounds. Our list of Fortune 500 clients included Turner Broadcasting Systems and Bell South Telecommunications.

As a result of my success, speaking engagements poured in. As I shared my story, a common thread defined what "success" meant to me. That common thread was the "Bruce" story. Bruce walked into our office ostensibly ready for job placement after completing a government-backed word processing training program but looking like he belonged anywhere else. His attire was wrinkled and crumpled, as if he had stumbled in after barely surviving the tornadoes, hurricanes and hailstorms of life.

Bruce looked at the floor when spoken to, his bowed head seemingly weighted down with disappointment after disappointment, and his eyes fixed on the neutrality and nonjudgment of objects in the room rather than making human eye contact. It seemed to me that Bruce was trying to hide his longing for acceptance and validation in a society that saw him only as someone it could exploit for profit, enrolling him in programs that would not serve him, just to get the government's money.

We gently broke the news to Bruce that, according to our assessment, his skills needed some upgrading; and we encouraged him to come as often as he liked to the office, to take advantage of free self-paced word processing training.

For the next year and a half, Bruce came religiously to the office each week to work on his skills. He wasn't cut out for office work, and he knew it, but he kept coming back because we accepted

---

I think Bruce found, in our office, what he needed more than a job, more than training: acceptance, love and a sense of family.

---

and loved him. And each week Bruce's stature appeared taller, the wrinkles in his attire seemed to smooth out a little more, his walk was more intentional, his smile grew more radiant. When I peered into the training room to say, "Hello, Bruce, nice to see you today," his smile lit up the room.

Oddly enough, Bruce never asked to be placed on an assignment using his word processing skills. Since we placed only clerical employees, he found a laborer's position. But still, he kept coming to weekly training. I think Bruce found, in our office, what he needed more than a job, more than training: acceptance, love and a sense of family.

Years later, here I was, in the same place Bruce had been in when he walked in our door that afternoon. I, too, needed validation, and after years of running myself ragged to get it, I had made myself sick from stress. But unlike Bruce, I had the equivalent of a post-graduate degree in the art of masking. I stood tall and immaculately attired, though inwardly I was bent with insecurity—my soul weighed down from decades of being the good girl who tried with all her heart to please everyone and could never succeed in that losing battle.

This practice caused me to mute my inner voice of self-acceptance and self-nurturing; it caused me to mute my instinct for self-love. Unconsciously, I placed my awakening—to the knowledge that God had created me—on hold and lived my precious life like a puppet, allowing anyone to control my movements in the hope of gaining his love and acceptance. Eventually, I ended up in the

---

In the years that followed, I came to realize that my "Bruce" story was my own story. I was Bruce.

---

hospital. (Later, I was diagnosed with Chronic Fatigue Syndrome, a condition that wasn't widely recognized in the mid-1990s.)

The mysterious illness was worrisome and inconvenient, and after two days, the doctor came to me and said, "We can't find anything wrong with you. I think you just need to de-stress your life. Take a break. Rest. You can go home tomorrow." *All that, and, "You can go home tomorrow?" Really?* Upon my release, I immediately disobeyed doctor's orders and returned to work. Working hard was so much a part of my life that I thought I would die without it. I *was* my business. I was what I achieved; no more, no less. And yet I had a nagging sense that I was headed in the wrong direction, chasing after shadows.

One night not long after I left the hospital, after I finished my nightly prayer, an indescribable peace fell on me. I heard God whispering in my ear, reassuring me. "You are my child, a miracle, created in my image. You are worthy!" When I heard that voice, my recovery—my transformation—began. In the years that followed, I came to realize that my "Bruce" story was my own story. I was Bruce.

Jesus said, "Truly I tell you, whatever you did for one of the least of these brothers and sisters of mine, you did for me," (Matthew 25:40). I had always tried to live by this message, giving "the least of these" a place at my table and in my heart. I had watched and become deeply invested in Bruce's transformation through love, acceptance and ultimately self-acceptance, but I'd forgotten—if I had indeed known before—that I was worthy of the same.

Formerly President of L.A. Fitts, Inc. DBA Dynamic People, Linda J. Davis is now a certified life coach and founder of Be the Miracle Every Day, a movement to experience the joy of living every day. During her career, Linda has been featured in two national publications, Franchising World *and* Black Enterprise, *for her success in the temporary staffing industry. She completed her bachelor's degree of applied studies in organizational leadership at Mercer University, and master's of divinity, with a concentration in Christian education, from McAfee School of Theology at Mercer University in Atlanta, Georgia. Connect with Linda at www. BeTheMiracleEveryDay.com.*

Terlisa Faye Brown Sheppard

Go Home, Quit Work and Get Your Life in Order

In the summer of 2001, I started experiencing a dull, aching, lower back pain that just would not go away. After about a month of steady pain, I went to my medical doctor, who examined me and came to the conclusion that I had a slight bladder infection.

The doctor gave me a prescription for antibiotics and sent me on my way. But then a couple of months went by, and the pain continued. *Something isn't right with this diagnosis,* I thought. *A slight bladder infection shouldn't last this long.*

Having already passed my two-year cancer-free marker from the breast cancer I'd been diagnosed with in 1998, I was sure: *It can't be cancer again.* But I felt my oncologist should know what was going on.

I went in for an exam and tests on a beautiful, crisp November day and brought my mother, my sister Dorothy and her husband Jay with me for support. Even so, I wasn't too worried until the moment when my doctor came into the room where we'd all been waiting for the test results and grasped my hands tightly in her own, looking deep into my eyes.

"This is not good, Terlisa," she said, in front of everyone. "You have stage four breast cancer, and it has metastasized to your bones, your lungs and your liver. Go home, quit work and get your affairs in order!"

Her words rang in my ears, piercing my soul. Blindsided, shocked, still holding her cool hands, I sat on the edge of the examination table waiting to hear some kind of explanation for what I had just heard. *Am I hearing her right?* I searched my doctor's eyes, but there was no hope there. My life was ending: she had just pronounced my death sentence. *But I'm doing so well! How can this be? What about Alexis and Alyah? They need me! I need them!* My beautiful, clueless little girls were only three and five. *I'm too young for this—I'm too young to die!*

As these thoughts raced through my head, I avoided eye contact with my family, knowing that if our eyes met I would break down, or they would, and then we'd all just cry and cry and cry. I felt as though I was suffocating, right there in front of everyone. So my family had to be strong for me once again. I thought back to the first time I'd been diagnosed with breast cancer—when I was eight

---

Her words rang in my ears, piercing my soul.

---

and a half months pregnant with my second child, my miracle baby, Alyah. I recalled those long, dreadful days, months, even years that I had fought through eight cycles of chemotherapy, five to six weeks of radiation at five days a week and then a left-breast mastectomy with immediate reconstructive surgery.

It started as just a small lump under my left arm between my breast and my armpit. My OB kept telling me it was milk ducts from my pregnancy—not to worry. But toward the end of my pregnancy, the lump grew and grew at an alarming rate. One afternoon I took a late lunch hour and went for a mammogram. The doctor who did my test seemed concerned and wanted to do a biopsy that same day. I never got back to work. At around seven o'clock in the evening, she came in, stood right in front of me and said, "Terlisa, it's cancer!"

As the surgeon described a recommended course of treatment, my whole body went numb with shock. *Cancer?* I immediately thought: *Death.* And then, *No! My unborn child—I just have to*

deliver her, and then I'll deal with whatever happens on my end.
"You won't be able to breastfeed," the surgeon said.

In my shock, I protested. I'd breastfed my daughter Alexis, now two, for nine months. "I need to breastfeed," I pleaded with the doctor. "I need to make sure my child gets a start."

"Terlisa, I don't think you understand. You'll be going through chemo and radiation. Breastfeeding will be impossible."

I had been at my doctor's office a long time. My close friend Debbie called. "Where are you? We've got to do our baby registry."

"Debbie," I said, "I have breast cancer." She gasped. I heard a sob on the other end of the line, and then she steadied her voice. "Faye, I'm so sorry."

"If I had one day left in my life, what would I do?"

In shock, I calmly asked, "Can you start the phone calls?" I floated numbly from the clinic and home to tell my husband. We'd been having some trouble, but he was right there for me. Distraught, he held me as we wept.

Just one week after the diagnosis, I gave birth early to my miracle baby, Alyah. The first moment I looked into her tiny face I thought, fiercely, "I'm going to get you through this no matter what."

I'd started scrapbooking before Alexis was born, to keep a record of my pregnancy and the life of our family, and I'd taken countless pictures of my little girl. I saved special documents, letters, cards and her first efforts at drawing, and I pasted them all into the scrapbooks. During my pregnancy with Alyah, I took pictures of my changing body and added those, too. The family record had blossomed and grown steadily for more than two years by the time Alyah came along.

When I got sick, I knew immediately that the scrapbook also had to become a kind of history, a journal, so that if anything happened to me, my daughters would know who I was and all about the early parts of their lives. I started adding everything, including materials related to my illness, charts, hospital bracelets, pictures of me before and after surgery. *Who knows how many days I have left on this earth?* And I added a sort of introduction page, a letter to both of them:

"If I had one day left in my life, what would I do? I'd spend it with you, my beloved Alexis and Alyah, holding you close and telling you how much I love you." But thankfully, I responded well to treatment, went into remission and embraced our second chance with all my heart.

And then came the shock of the second, dire diagnosis. This time, I was so sick, so weak and so drained from all of the poisonous toxins invading my body that I often believed the death sentence would come to pass. Weekly trips to MD Anderson Cancer Center were a must, and I'd never seen so many needles in my entire life. There were injections of Benadryl just before treatments, so my body could tolerate the harsh chemotherapy drugs; the chemo drugs, injected into a port in my chest; and the subsequent injections of anti-nausea medicines. Following that cycle, I endured painful injections to my abdomen to boost my failing white blood counts. Many times I thought, *How much pain can one person really take in her lifetime?*

Days were planned around dispensing and taking my incredible number of medications, and I was too sick to perform what were once daily routines. Sometimes I didn't even remember waking up or how I got in the shower. Sores began to form in my mouth, which made my small appetite even worse. As the weeks passed, though I kept trying to be strong for everyone else, I became depressed. My whole family rallied around me to help, but sometimes, in my lowest moments, I thought, *I'm not going to make it.*

But then I'd pick up the scrapbook I always had nearby and page through it. I'd look at the sonograms from when I was pregnant with the girls, their baby pictures, their first birthdays—I looked at that record of the growth of our happiness and realized I had to regain control of my life and not let my disease defeat me. There were cards and pictures and little items, too, that were waiting to

126

be added to the scrapbook. There were so many things I needed to write down. And the girls were growing so fast…

I became determined to fight the cancer: *I will not give up. I will not accept a death sentence.* And over the next couple of months, I began to regain my strength. I began to look at my illness in a new light and to read and understand more and more about it each day. With a new, bright fire in my belly, I studied ways of eating and drinking that could boost my health. Breast cancer was just a part of me, not my life. *I have a life to live, and I am determined to live*

I am thriving day to day with a cancerous tumor in my brain.

---

it to the fullest, no matter what happens. No more stagnation! I am not a sick person—I am a wife, a mother, a daughter, a sister and a friend. I mean a lot to those around me. I have to adjust my attitude and stand up to this cancer!

Again, I went into remission. And I was later diagnosed with cancer a third time in August of 2003. This time, it metastasized to my brain. Again, a defeatist spirit entered my mind and body. But after having my moment, I proceeded to prepare myself for a grueling, painful eight-hour strategic surgery that would shrink my brain tumor through a very high dose of radiation. I am thriving day to day with a cancerous tumor in my brain. Yes, God has a purpose for me! For eight years now, the tumor has pretty much remained stable.

I don't have to give up on life just because someone tells me I'm sick. In fact, I never will. That's just their story, and if I believed the death sentence would be fulfilled, well, then, that would be the outcome.

Now I talk to survivors all over the world, encouraging them to fight, letting them know that they don't have to accept death as their only outcome for a cancer diagnosis. I carry my scrapbook with me everywhere I go; I take it on the road, I take it to cancer centers. It continues to help me to fight and mark my daughters' growing up.

My fifteen-year-old, Alexis, is as tall as I am now! Alyah is thirteen and not far behind her. They take care of themselves very well.

I show the scrapbook to other patients at the clinic where I get chemo, and I often kid with my nurses and tell them I'm practicing medicine without a license. One time my nurse actually had me go, pushing my pole, to another patient's room. She had just been diagnosed with a brain tumor, as I had been earlier.

Since I am a firm believer in "look-good, feel-better," I dress up for my chemo treatments from head to toe: stilettos, the whole nine yards. So when I walked in the patient's room to talk to her about my experience with a cancerous brain tumor and what I do to keep it together, she just gave me this look like, "Aww, you don't understand."

I went back to my room, got my scrapbook, brought it back to her and flipped through the pages showing the period when I had my brain surgery. When she saw my story come to life, and how much we had in common, I felt her open right up to me. And I could feel her open up to hope for the future.

We *can* fight through this. We can live with cancer.

Terlisa Faye Brown Sheppard is a breast cancer survivor of thirteen years and counting. Her mission is to encourage and motivate other cancer survivors to "live" through their diagnosis and to enjoy each and every day on this earth. She is currently at work on her first book. Connect with Terlisa at www.HelpingFightBreastCancer.com.

Janna Waldinger

This Is It

I magine waking up in the middle of a dream. It's dark outside. I'm in the front passenger seat of a small car traveling on a mountain road. I feel the heavy presence of the mountain wall on my left side, vulnerability as I glance at the sheer drop of the cliff to my right. Suddenly the man driving the car drives right off the road. I'm suspended in midair. "This is it!" The words land in my heart as I realize there is no longer any road beneath me.

I wake up in shock, with the adrenaline, fear and sheer amazement of the free fall still surging through my body. But more pronounced than those physical sensations is my sudden awakening. *This is it!* I'm twelve years old, and I get it. I get it; life is no joke. We are not here just for the entertainment. Everything counts! Everything is important. It is time to get my life in order. There is no time to lose. The dream's life-changing message shows me that waking time and dreamtime, every moment, merits conscious investigation.

Ever since that "I get it" moment, I have known that I am here to seize the moment, to show up and shine. At a very young age, even long before my dream, I began to explore beyond the seen world to find a sense of wholeness. My photography-loving father trained me to make art of the world: the direction of light as it falls upon a scene; the depth of the shadows that define my perspective; and an awareness of spatial relations of foreground, middle ground and background. From my social worker mother, I acquired a yearning to understand people, to be of service and to make a difference in the world. No one ever tried to convince me that I couldn't make a difference.

In 1990, the Velvet Revolution occurred in the Czech Republic, a non-violent revolution that offered hope and a chance to revision the future for the Czech people. At that time I was the Executive Director of the Institute For Living Arts (IFLA), a concept-driven,

Ever since that "I get it" moment, I have known that I am here to seize the moment, to show up and shine.

socially conscious arts organization. Lowell Downey, my partner in love and life, was the Program Director, and we were thrilled to be invited by the Lindhart's Foundation and Karl Srp of ArtForum to bring the first ecological art exhibition from the United States to Prague.

We assembled a group of artists to create *Art of Ecology— Recycling the Collective Spirit,* a collaborative art exhibition to support the sudden, powerful emergence of information and innovation now being shared between artists, scientists and politicians.

My heart raced with the determination to use whatever influence we had to create a safe place for dialogue on environmental issues and try to guide the new government in paying serious attention to ecological issues.

But some highly placed people did not want us in Prague. Before we left for Prague, we received a phone call from our host telling us that our exhibition had been canceled. We found that some "powerful forces" were opposed to our visit. We knew very well that the country was in flux. Authority had broken down. Were these powerful opponents part of the old regime—a regime that made people disappear with impunity? People had been jailed for speaking out about ecology and environmental responsibility. Would this project cost us our lives?

Now, as Lowell and I prepared for our journey into the unknown, we gathered around a friend's fireplace for a ritual of protection. I was fearful but determined. As our friend placed a mystical net of safety around us, I could see past the anxiety. We would go. We would help open the possibility that artists and visionaries, who had been oppressed for generations, could take on the leadership of their country. We would show them that they were not alone and that their struggle was being witnessed.

When we arrived, Prague was in a state of total change and reinvention. Civil servants were not being paid, and services were nonexistent or suspended. Policemen weren't willing to risk their lives for the very small salary they were being paid. After

---

But some highly placed people
did not want us in Prague.

---

years of being told just what to do and when to do it, people were confused and unsure of the extent of their authority. The notion that individuals could shape their daily lives and contribute to a hopeful future was slowly sinking in.

The old rules no longer applied, but they stuck anyway. For example: When we arrived, bakeries and shops were not open on Saturday or Sunday, just as under the Communist regime. By the time we left, six weeks later, new entrepreneurs had broken this mold and were open on weekends with businesses that they themselves owned. Visionary artists were rushing in to take hold of new possibilities to birth this new freedom and give creative license for the young and old to experiment.

The artists we worked with were wonderful; the environmentalists we met were friendly and glad to exchange with us. However, every step was a challenge. For example, we needed a catalog for the exhibit but spent many days simply tracking down the machines and paper needed to produce it. Publicizing an art exhibition was something that, previously, would have been totally overseen and controlled by the government. People did not yet have the basic material resources at hand to give expression to their new dreams and ideals. The Czech Republic was definitely a work in progress.

Getting permission to do *anything* was a challenge. Wild and wonderful things were happening in Prague. No one was sure who was in charge or what the new rules were. Officials said "no" to everything out of a holdover fear from the Soviet regime. Those who felt they might overstep uncertain bounds or break an

---

Twenty years later I find myself once again in a world of revolution.

---

unknowable rule thought they would surely be punished. I learned to shift the "no" into a "yes" by asking a simple question: "Who can say yes?" Immediately the person who had been stuck in the "no" was free to tell me who could say that magic word.

The psychological aspects were far more difficult than the inconveniences of bureaucracy and scarcity. I was cautious, always looking over my shoulder, wondering if our project was at risk as I confronted anti-Semitism, fear and lies. It is a shock to travel to a culture where the law had long been the enemy.

A sense of freedom was in the air, alongside a bitter sense of distrust and concern. It was still unclear who could be trusted. I didn't sleep well. I was on edge stretching what was possible. And I constantly wondered, *Am I safe?*

I had doubts about my own work. I was used to making miniature glass and steel sculptures. Now I was working with the master glass artist, Vaslav Borovicka, on six-foot-by-twelve-foot sandblasted glass panels in his studio a hundred kilometers outside of Prague. *Who do I think I am? Will I fall flat on my face?*

But I couldn't quit. I was invigorated, filled with a sense of purpose. We had come with a goal that was far bigger than our fear: To bring art that would inspire the people to speak up and demand a new direction for the newly forming country, to demand clean air, clean water and clean energy as basic human rights. And we were needed. *This is it!* I felt it—we all did. *I have to keep going. I might have to look over my shoulder, but I will keep walking forward.*

Against all odds, *Art of Ecology – Recycling the Collective Spirit* was a success and well attended. The gallery was a converted stable in old secret service headquarters at the foot of Prague Castle. It was the beginning of a bridge between art and ecology that had not existed before in Prague. One of the works was "Hopewell," by Daniel DiPerro. This open suitcase engaged and inspired people to place poems and drawings that symbolized their dreams for the future in it.

No fear of repression could hold us back. Instead, it helped to fuel our action to channel our dream to contribute to healing the world. This was it—this was a door we were going to open on a global scale.

Twenty years later I find myself once again in a world of revolution. People everywhere are finding their enough button and making changes. My strength is sourced by an unyielding drive, a calling from my soul. Every day, I awaken committed to a passion for life that leads me towards the beautiful unknown. I am giving myself permission to dream a dream that connects me to my emerging voice in the midst of uncertainty.

Janna Waldinger earned her BA in sculpture at the College of Creative Studies of the University of California at Santa Barbara. For the past twenty years, Janna's multi-media photography and video company, Art & Clarity, has provided her clients with successful creative solutions and imagery. Her son, Forest, inspired her children's book, Finding the Door to Sleep. *She serves as an elected official on the Napa County Board of Education, where she contributes an artistic, out-of-the-box perspective. She is available for speaking engagements. To find out about her Napa Valley retreats, connect and engage her photography and video services at www.ArtandClarity.com and www.MakeArtOfMDay.com.*

Deliaya York

A Vow to Smile

As I stood in the chapel of the ancient monastery in beautiful upstate New York, awaiting my ordination into the life of a minister, images suddenly flooded into my mind, images of that moment eleven years ago when I was struck by lightning and was literally, in a flash, transformed forever.

On that night I was standing on a balcony, high in a building, wearing headphones, when the lightning struck. Using the headphones as a conductor, the lightning entered my ear and then traveled down through my body, scorching every internal organ that lay in its path. I could hear the crackling of my own flesh as it coursed through me. The pain was so raw and intense that I kept touching my head, expecting to find blood or a piece of my skull in my hand.

The path that the lightning took was unmistakable, for it remained on fire in my body. I was suddenly profoundly aware that I had a right and left side of my brain; both sides no longer coexisted. Similarly, my entire body was split down the center with a distinct right and left side to everything. I could feel a single nerve in my arm on one side of my body while feeling an equal and opposite nerve on the other side. Alarmingly, they were presently not doing the same thing; one half of my body felt numb and tingling, the other unresponsive. My brain had gone haywire.

A loud ringing reverberated through my head. I felt as if I was in a torture chamber, locked in a tiny room while an incessant gong clanged next to my head. I was uncomfortably cold, freezing. Suddenly I was at the hospital. The wheelchair in the emergency room felt like the Teacups at Disneyland. I asked the attendant to please stop for a moment because I thought I was going to vomit.

He replied, "Ma'am, we're not moving."

I had one thought in what what was left of my mind: *I'm fucked.*

Suddenly, all the muscles in my body seemed to change from solid to fluid. I began sliding out of the wheelchair onto the hospital floor. The fluorescent lights on the ceiling flickered. I could see

---

I kept touching my head, expecting to find blood or a piece of my skull in my hand.

---

only a portion of everything; my eyes rolled back in my head, the muscles behind them aching from their fixed, unnatural position. My head smacked the cold, hard, hopefully sanitary, hospital floor.

I heard the nurses asking each other, "What's happening to her?" Not what I wanted to hear from my professional attendants.

Then, as if somebody flipped a switch, every cell in my body contracted, causing me to contort like a pretzel; my toes curled, my knees locked, my back arched, my fingernails dug into my head. I felt moisture. I later learned the moisture was blood from the gouges my nails had left in my scalp.

My consciousness began to diminish in effort to escape the torment. I welcomed oblivion. To my dismay, just as I approached this blissful nothingness, my body's convulsing subsided, leaving me trapped in the awareness of my current reality. A couple minutes later the contractions resumed. The toggling of these two states went on for hours and about every third day for the next eight years of my life. In an instant the life that I knew was gone, and I was thrust into a life that was foreign and unwanted.

As the years passed, I became increasingly fearful of falling asleep at night, for each morning brought the discovery of a new loss. Each day new parts of myself became unrecognizable. The person that I knew myself to be was rapidly slipping away.

The doctors said that my brain cells were slowly dying. It was unfathomable, horrifying. I was experiencing the dissolution of my own mind. I fought urgently to hold onto it. Hour-by-hour, day-by-day, it dissolved, each time a little more of me slipping

---

In an instant the life that I knew was gone.

---

away into a mysterious chamber that I could not open. I struggled with every ounce of strength I had to hang onto the girl I knew, but it was to no avail, and finally, one day I woke-up and realized that she was nowhere to be found.

Months passed, and I struggled to make sense of my new existence. Again, the challenge was too much to handle. And then one day, alone in my house, the familiar pain in my chest hit me like a tornado; my brain began its usual sequence of shutting down and going into a seizure. I hit the floor.

This time was different. My body was doing the usual erratic convulsing, followed by a completely unresponsive state, however, my brain continued convulsing without the comatose reprieve. I felt the blood pulsing through my entire head and neck and down into my shoulders. I believed I was dying.

I don't know if you can actually feel blood vessels, but if you can, mine hurt. The combination of a limp, lifeless body and a brain that was convulsing like an exposed electrical wire was almost too much to bear. Part of me was okay with this knowledge that I was dying because I knew it would stop the torture in my head. Apparently a larger part of me wanted to live because somehow, before I hit the floor, I dialed 911.

Through the dangling receiver I heard a voice asking if I was okay.

"No," I said in my mind. I lay there watching the blurry receiver of the phone sway back and forth until either it stopped or I did. I heard a pounding on my glass door. Two deputies entered my house. I heard them searching through my rooms, looking for the caller of the non-responsive 911 call. I couldn't call out and tell them where I was. They found me in the last place they looked.

"Thank God," I thought, "Maybe I still have a chance."

The paramedics arrived and hoisted me down the stairs and onto the gurney. The bumping sent my body into further physical distress. The paramedic slammed the doors shut, and we were off.

I was safe and ready for the next challenge.

With each bump I felt less able to handle what I was experiencing. My brain could neither process a thought nor produce one. All I could do was to "be." I simply existed. Life had no apparent significance, though I fought to stay in it.

Then suddenly everything stopped. I had no more pain. All was silent. A peacefulness enveloped me. Everything went from a dark, hazy gray to a brilliant white. I never knew light could be that white. Through the brilliance came the most angelic music. I heard the sweet sound of loving voices within the glorious music. Somehow the voices were familiar even though I could not see them. The voices were filled with love and an excitement for my arrival. And amazingly, I was excited, too. I realized I missed them, even though I was not sure exactly who they were.

The whiteness of the light expanded to include me in its embrace. I felt sparkles all around me. I was delighted and dazzled. Just when the light grew large enough to fully hold me in its magnificence, I realized that I was in the upper, back part of the ambulance looking down. I saw my body lying on the gurney, the paramedics hovering over me.

I watched them prepare the IV, stretching the plastic tube that extends from the bag to the needle. I noticed the large size of the needle and knew that if I were in my body I would be dreading its insertion. I saw the back of my hand as though it were close-up. I watched in slow motion as the paramedic jammed the needle hard into the back of my hand, piercing my tender skin. In that moment

I experienced an awareness of just how fragile the human body truly is.

I looked over to the bright light that beckoned me to enter. I knew now that our existence in mankind could end in an instant. I looked back at my body lying in the back of the ambulance. For the first time ever, I thought I was pretty.

As I marveled at myself with untarnished eyes, I saw a beauty I had never seen before. All judgments of my self vanished. My face looked so peaceful, like a porcelain doll. My hair tousled, but still softly, gently framing my innocent face. My body was gorgeous. My limbs and organs were all put together with a masterful, mystical technology. I was mesmerized at how I lay there apparently still alive. An appreciation for my life filled my soul to overflowing. In that instant, I fell in love with myself. I wanted to live.

I looked back at the brilliant, sparkling white light. The beings within the light already knew of my choice to live. I heard one jokester among the crowd yell, "We'll see ya when ya come back!" His words struck me to the core. This whole life was a choice. I choose when to incarnate and I choose when to die.

I realized that there was another part of me running the show. A part that was eternal. It was my soul. I asked the Source of the Light, "Please let me remember this when I return."

The Source answered, "Yes, you will remember what you need to remember." I believe it was God. For a moment that seemed to last an eternity I allowed myself to be held in the arms of that Presence. Never have I felt so safe or unconditionally loved and accepted.

"Smack!" I felt the handsome paramedic's powerful hands pumping my chest. I gasped and re-entered my body through a hole about an inch and a half in diameter at my sternum. The sudden pain shocked my system. My body felt so heavy, cumbersome.

I wondered for a moment if I had made the right choice. But then I sensed the brilliant, sparkling white light traveling around and within me. I noticed it surrounding both paramedics too. And I knew all was well. I was unchangeable, yet forever changed. A deep gratitude warmed my entire body, and I knew that I was safe and ready for the next challenge.

Back at the monastery it suddenly all became clear: all those challenges, all that pain had simply been preparing me for this moment. Everything in this glorious, messy, beautiful, ever-changing world is an opportunity for me to learn and to love. This place that we call earth is the perfect place to grow a heart filled to overflowing with compassion and kindness. My life is a gift.

I stepped onto the altar and spoke my vows: *I vow to be a beacon of love, light, joy and hope through which Divine love flows. I vow to savor each moment as a precious gift, knowing that Life is now. I vow to forgive myself and others when we fall short. I vow to smile.*

Deliaya York is an inspirational and transformational speaker, minister and homemaker. A lightning strike and traumatic brain injury survivor, she shares her remarkable story with others in the hope that they, too, will take the risk and accept their calling.

Loretta (LaRue') Duncan-Fowler

Fighting for
Something Greater

W hen we touched down in California in August of 1984, I
kissed the ground. I was ready to spread my wings and
fly, with my three children, as a newly single mother in the land
of milk and honey, leaving pain and hardship behind—or so I
thought.

The first month in Sacramento was idyllic. My childhood
friend, Eva, and her husband, Joe, met us at the airport and helped
us get acclimated. Within two weeks I had a townhouse apartment
with a swimming pool, beautiful green grass and flowers outside.
Everyone was so nice and friendly! I was shedding my provincial
Bostonian ways and meeting new people. I loved being the new kid
on the block.

Once we were settled in our new place, I enrolled my children in
school. It was easy with Dawn; she was bright and articulate, wise
beyond her seven years. Noel was still too young to go to school.
As for my beloved first son, Raymond, whom we affectionately call
Ray Ray, I had to make a special plan for him, Special Education's
Individual Educational Placement (IEP) Assessment, which
determined the correct placement for a child with disabilities.

The IEP team, which consisted of me, Ray Ray's special education
teacher and his physical, occupational and speech therapists, had
decided the correct placement for him was at the Ethel Phillips

Elementary School in the Sacramento School District. I had done my research well, and I knew—or thought I knew—all the state and federal laws pertaining to my particular situation. Ray Ray had been in early intervention programs since he was eight months old.

I was determined to give Ray Ray—to give all of my kids—the best life possible. We'd had Ray Ray in physical, occupational and speech therapy for three years after the first doctors gave us the news: they didn't expect Ray Ray to live more than a year, with his rare and devastating condition, as anything but a vegetable. Still more vivid than any other was the memory of Ray Ray lying on

My life had just changed in a sound byte.

the bed, happy and gurgling in his little blue and white seersucker onesie, as his father played reggae tunes—and the sudden, terrible jerking of his tiny head, his lips turning blue. I had prayed, speaking almost in tongues, all the way to the hospital, fighting for my baby's life in the spirit realm.

We had triumphed, and Ray Ray was thriving; but I still felt like I had a lot to prove to my God, myself and my family, who were not very supportive of me moving three thousand miles away with three small children and no husband. Sometimes we were a little homesick, but I had bought one-way tickets, and I was determined to be successful in our new home. So far, our transition was going smoothly, even beautifully.

Trouble came knocking on our door the evening of Ray Ray's official enrollment in his first school. As I was preparing dinner and the kids were watching their favorite sitcom, I heard the shouting and angry voices of the people on the screen as I turned around: "NEWS FLASH! After a special meeting held at the Ethel Phillips Elementary School in Sacramento, parents are picketing and protesting today's enrollment of a four year-old child at the school in their Special Education class. It appears that the family relocated from Boston, Massachusetts, one month ago, and the child has cytomegalovirus (CMV), a rare disease that is similar to HIV, the disease that causes AIDS. Parents are outraged at his enrollment." My life had just changed in a sound byte.

At first it didn't dawn on me that they were talking about *my* family. I didn't know what CMV was, and the doctors in Boston never really put a name on what caused Raymond's condition. But I certainly knew what AIDS was. It was running rampant across

---

I didn't have time for rage—I went straight into survival mode.

---

the country and the world, and the stigma was horrendous. As I gravitated to the television, I gathered what was happening. It was *my* family they were talking about. My legs gave out and I sat on the floor in shock, holding my babies close. I didn't know there were tears on my face until Dawn said, "Mommy, you're crying."

Staring at the screen, I realized that my idyllic California dream was turning into a nightmare. And it was being played out on local television. I couldn't believe the outrage and the anger on the parents' faces—it was a serious mob. I felt a wave of fear begin to engulf me. Just then the phone rang, and I rushed to pick it up, keeping my eyes glued to the TV. It was the Superintendent of schools, calling to warn me about what had just transpired.

"You're too late," I said, choking back my tears. "I've already seen the news."

The Superintendent and I decided to meet the next morning to discuss what was happening. He would send a car to pick me up, and it was suggested that I find childcare for Ray Ray instead of bringing him with me, since parents would be returning the next day to continue picketing, and they didn't want Raymond or me to be harmed—although it was within my rights to send him to school on the little yellow bus that was supposed to start picking him up tomorrow.

I didn't have time for rage—I went straight into survival mode. My first thought was to protect my children. This was home for me, and I was going to fight tooth and nail to live here. They didn't know who they were messing with! I politely thanked the Superintendent for his concern and told him I would be ready.

When I arrived at the school that morning, the picket lines were in full swing, and the parents were angry and voicing their concerns loudly. I was whisked into the school as news cameras and lights flashed. I was twenty-three and looked fifteen when I had attended our first IEP meeting, but when I opened my mouth now I spoke the King's English so no one could stereotype me as

---

Finally, Ray Ray and I won our victory,
and he was able to go to school.

---

a single, unmarried black woman. As liberal as California seems to be, the racism here was covert and insidious, and I picked up on it right away, so I made sure to be sharp as a tack in my suit, stockings and heels. I wanted them to know I meant business. I had put on the whole armor of God, and I was ready for the fight of Ray's and my life.

The Superintendent explained that Raymond's special education teacher was pregnant and was afraid of contracting CMV, which was then, like HIV, thought to be highly contagious. She didn't want to harm her unborn baby, so she didn't want to teach Ray. When the school board suggested she take an early maternity leave, it must have ticked her off: She notified the parents and called the press, and they had an emergency meeting right after I left the IEP meeting. Everything had literally changed in a matter of hours.

Over the next two years, I would fight for my son Raymond Austin Duncan to attend the Sacramento Public Schools. The Center for Disease Control (CDC) in Atlanta was called in; I started doing the rounds of local television, and our family was in the paper every day. I received everything from death threats to crazy healing remedies and had to change our phone number several times. Our neighborhood was small, and soon everyone knew our business. I lost friends because people didn't want my children to play with their children. "You can come over," they might say, "but not Ray Ray." Or, "There's too much drama in your life." My family was too far away to really understand my struggle. Even my best friend Eva changed.

Many nights I cried and raged. But when I prayed I found the answer: *It's not about you. This is about Ray Ray—and beyond that, it's for a higher purpose.* I always knew I had been called by God to be my children's mother. Now I discovered I was here to serve that higher purpose. Even when it got really, really bad, I thought, *This is going to make a difference in someone's life. I'm going to use it as a platform.*

Parents took their children out of the school in droves, and the school started to lose federal funding because of the absences of the other children. When that happened, I was forced to home-school Ray Ray, who still needed all of his therapy programs. I was only able to perform the rudimentary ones like stretching exercises. He was still unable to walk.

An attorney from the Advocates for Children and Adults with Disabilities agreed to take my case, and our story gained momentum and national exposure when I appeared on *Nightline* with Ted Koppel, along with the CDC in Atlanta, under a pseudonym (I still needed to find work and I was counting on not everyone watching the program).

Eventually the court ruled that it was illegal to deny Ray Ray access. Two years of media hoopla had made it clear to our community that CMV was *not* HIV, and besides, it was unlawful for the schools to discriminate against a child with disabilities. Finally, Ray Ray and I won our victory, and he was able to go to school. Today, at thirty-one, he's doing great. He's a winsome, handsome guy with a pure heart.

When Ray Ray and I fought for his right to an education, I was young and somewhat naïve. I knew how to be a good wife and a good mother, as I'd been raised. But I didn't know before all this happened that I could speak. Fighting for Ray Ray gave me a voice. I didn't know how strong I was, how compassionate.

Everyone has some strength, something inside of them that makes them a champion. It's not about you; your fight is always about something greater. No matter what you go through in life, you can do whatever you put your mind to; and if hardship comes, God always provides a way.

Loretta (La-Rue') Duncan-Fowler is an author, singer, songwriter and performance poet. Her debut book, My Deepest Affections are Yours— Love Poems, received wide recognition. La-Rue' is a member of the performing groups Born 2 Be Poets, 2nd Born and Uptown Poets. She hosts her own spoken word show, An Evening of Poetry w/Ms. La-Rue', and the Mood Blue's Poetry Series. Born 2 Be Poets was nominated for the 2001 SOS Music Award in the Spoken Word Category. Spoken word is La-Rue's ministry gift, and she uses it to counteract the effects of hopelessness, depression and despair found in people today. She has graced the stage with Grammy Award-winning, Blues Hall of Fame and world music artists from The Whispers to Mr. Big John Evans to Goapele. She also wrote and recorded the song "Wretched Man" with notable gospel and blues guitarist Odell Ross Jr. Whether it's hosting a Katrina benefit or organizing community events to inform people about H1N1 and related health issues, you can find La-Rue' lecturing and lending her gift of poetry to civic, governmental, religious and charitable organizations. La-Rue' has appeared as a guest on Nightline with Ted Koppel, and several local talk shows including Look Who's Talking and Good Day Sacramento, advocating for the rights of her disabled son. She lives in Sacramento, CA. Connect with La-Rue' at www.LorettaLaRueDuncanFowler.com and www. LorettaLaRueDuncanFowler.info.

Jelani Hamm

Our Future Selves
Are Calling

W hen I first saw the police lights flashing in my rear view mirror it was like watching a horror movie that happened to be starring me. The detachment was surreal. It quickly became real when they clamped the handcuffs on me.

"When we ran your license plate, we found an arrest warrant out for you. You didn't pay a ticket for a moving violation, boy," the officer said. This can't be. I was a law-abiding citizen, highly educated, a Los Angeles schoolteacher and now I was going to jail for an unpaid traffic ticket?

The officers roughly shoved me into the police car. As they brought me through the processing line at the station, the shame and humiliation numbed me.

Everyone was staring at me, all the criminals, all the clerks, all the officers. Suddenly I was just another statistic, a black man who had broken the law and was now going to jail. Everything I had worked so hard to be vanished. In its place was someone I did not recognize.

When I moved to Los Angeles in the early 1980s, I was a young man filled with promise and ambition. I had just graduated with a music degree from the University of the Pacific in Northern California and was set to begin my graduate studies in theatre at California State University. I was no longer that country boy from

Georgia, the youngest of eight who had tasted the bitter sting of racism, family struggles and hard economic times.

My parents had given everything to send me to school in California, and I was determined to make them proud. Soon after, I had started a second master's in film producing from UCLA and began working as a schoolteacher. Yet I couldn't shake the mounting frustrations and disappointments.

Deep into my thirties, having experienced professional disappointment after professional disappointment, endless doors closing one after the other, doubt and worry became my norm. I was stuck. I was teaching to pay the bills and keep a roof over my head. I was good at what I did, but I wanted to act, to perform

Everything I had worked so hard
to be vanished. In its place was
someone I did not recognize.

and to create. The minor roles I got weren't enough; I was always struggling to pay my rent, constantly complaining to my brothers and sisters about one disaster after another. I was utterly lost.

The final hammer-blow to my self-esteem was the arrest and my night in jail. Suddenly, I started having panic attacks. My thoughts were filled with embarrassment and shame. My mind was filled with irrational fears of cops and helicopters. I no longer believed in myself. Doubt and worry blocked my vision.

After two years of this endless nightmare I made the decision to change. I no longer wanted to be the traditional Catholic, the black man from Georgia, the country boy. "I want to discover the Africa inside of me. I'm going to change my name, change my very being, start over, push the reset button," I declared.

I began reading books, talking to spiritual masters, anything that could help me find this new name, this new me. During this period, I met one of my greatest teachers, a man named Joseph. During one of our meditations, he introduced me to a Wise Old Man. He described a generous man who had traveled around the world, spoke many languages, gathered people together, performed, taught and wrote. I suddenly got the chills. He was my future self, and though he was only in our heads, created from our vision of what's possible, I could feel this man's presence. I began to write to him daily in my journals.

And then one morning I woke up, opened one of the many books I'd been reading, and saw the word "Jelani." It was a word that meant "mighty in spirit in several languages." This was the name! And yet, who was I to take such a name? *Who do you think you are?* I asked myself. To answer this question, to claim the name

---

*He was my future self, and though
he was only in our heads, created
from our vision of what's possible, I
could feel this man's presence.*

Jelani, I knew I had to do something big. I found my inspiration in the most unlikely of places. As a child, during the difficult times, I always escaped to the world of television. My favorite performer had always been Lucille Ball. I remembered an episode wherein Lucy and Ethel had jumped from an airplane. That's what I was going to do! It would be the leap that would start my new life.

I remember the day clearly. It was May 7, 1993, two days before my birthday. Alone, I drove out into the Mojave Desert. I didn't tell anyone what I was going to do. When I arrived, I felt calm and cool, ready for anything. That tranquility was quickly replaced by pure terror as I sat in the hangar and watched the video presentation of people jumping out of airplanes to the sounds of James Brown's "I Feel Good."

Walking out to the landing strip with my tandem partner I felt my heart rise into my throat and stick there. When we crawled into the tiny plane and it took off I noticed that the door was still open. *Where was the seatbelt?*

When we reached 11,000 feet and it was finally time to jump, I couldn't breathe, I couldn't move. No way could I do this! My tandem partner told me to breathe, to relax. Eventually, I felt a deep calm wash over me, and I heard the Wise Old Man inside me saying, "This is your first step to manhood."

We jumped. The noise and force of the wind in my face and ears was overpowering. All I could do was surrender to the moment. I was too scared to move; my partner pulled the parachute cord, and I could hear the hush of heaven. All I could say was, "Oh, my God!" over and over again. My partner joined in the refrain and it carried us down to the ground.

As my feet hit the earth it was like a jolt back to reality. On the drive back to Los Angeles, I was filled with a euphoric feeling, as if I'd pushed myself into another spiritual plane, but most importantly I knew I had earned the name Jelani, for I was truly, now, mighty in spirit.

On May 9, two days later, I had my name changing ceremony in a beautiful park in the Santa Monica Mountains. My teacher, Joseph, officiated at the ceremony. Some friends played African drums. At one point my friend Julie stood up and showed me a certificate. She told me she was adopting me as her brother and that it had been certified by the city of Los Angeles and witnessed by angels. It was a magnificent celebration. I had finally created the "me" that was always within me.

I realized that I had been living someone else's bad dream. My future self had been calling out to be magnificent. I had finally answered the call. From that day forward, I dedicated myself to being Jelani, allowing myself to honor both the magical little boy of my past and the Old Man of my future.

I began to travel. On my first trip to Paris, I felt truly American for the first time. In America I was the black man who might steal your purse. But in Paris I was Jelani. The freedom was exhilarating. I began to travel to Africa regularly. I became a student of French, Spanish, Swahili and Arabic. I began to fill my journals with travel stories and life essays.

My teaching began to take on a whole new meaning. I began concentrating on children with special needs. I began writing children's stories. I'm in the process of opening a school for young children of color who have difficulties in school.

Life has become fuller and more meaningful. I realized that the things we think are difficult are actually gifts. I learned that all the pains and heartaches are only portals through which we find our true selves, if we are brave enough to walk through those doors. By looking within myself, I often ask the Wise Old Man, "What next?" All the answers are found in the stillness within.

In 2006, I climbed Mount Kilimanjaro in Tanzania. Every step was arduous, but my new focus and thirst for adventure kept me on track. In my youth I had been a marathon runner, but this was something entirely different, a test, another call to be magnificent.

Each day I jump, spread my wings and
surrender to the man that I'm becoming.

At one point during the six-day journey my guide noticed I was laboring intensely to breathe, so we stopped to rest. I remember staring up at the nighttime sky. It was like looking at a blanket of black velvet dotted with shimmering diamonds. Lost in the magnificence of that moment I heard my inner voice say, *Go home.*

We descended without going to the summit and went back to the campsite. During the night I passed out and my blood pressure dropped dangerously low. I almost died.

While I did not make it to the summit, I reached a height even greater: the wisdom to listen to the still, small voice within. I never would have had the opportunity to behold such a sight if I hadn't pushed myself to the limit. This was something my old self could never have done, but for Jelani, it was like breathing air.

Since then, I have repurposed the flashing lights of my past and blessed the unfortunate series of circumstances that landed me at rock bottom. The police lights were the lights and cameras to capture my attention. Today, I am starring in my own movie, for which I am the director and creative writer. Unlike Lucille Ball, I make no cuts and retakes. Each day is a new and exhilarating scene, full of fresh possibilities and breakthroughs. Each day I jump, spread my wings and surrender to the man that I'm becoming.

Jelani Hamm earned his bachelor's of music from the University of the Pacific, an MA in theater from California State University, LA and an MFA in film producing from UCLA. He is currently completing his PhD in world arts and culture from UCLA. He is a credentialed education specialist and continues to work with special needs children in the Los Angeles public schools. His first series of children's books will be released in the fall of 2011, and a collection of travel adventures and life essays are soon to be published in a book, Frolicking on the Edge of the World. *Connect with Jelani at www.OneAfricanVillage.com, JelaniOnline.com or BurkeStreetPress.com.*

Jeunesse Hosein, JD

A New Legacy: A Mother's Journey Back to Love

The call came from neighbors I barely knew. "Your daughter is here. She's all right, but she walked home from school." I told them I would be right there and rushed home. It had been a hectic morning, getting six year-old Meera ready for school, getting myself ready for work. A bus ride to the school, and I dreaded being late.

Alighting from the bus with the school in sight just ahead, I told her to walk the rest of the way by herself and went on my way to work. Instead, she walked home. All the way. By herself.

Back in our tiny bachelor's apartment, I spanked her. I was an automaton; I felt nothing. Not anger, not fear, nothing. Afterward, memories of my own childhood came flooding back, and I was horrified at myself. *I spanked my child. I let her walk alone to school. She had to turn to strangers for help. I put her in danger. And just days ago, a child in our neighborhood was kidnapped and killed.* All that was true. But deeper and stronger were the thoughts that had nagged at me for months now. Sick with guilt and terror, I finally had to acknowledge: *I no longer feel any emotional connection with my daughter. I am not fit to be her mother.*

I had become what I never wanted to be—like my mother. My grandmother had raised me with loving care until I was about four. When she died, all the love was gone from my life. I felt so abandoned. Up until Meera was about four years old herself, I was a terrific mother. But after that, I started to shut down. My own mother, Edith, was neglectful. When my siblings and I came home from school, she would usually be in bed. We would set about cooking dinner.

My mother never gave me a sense of being protected and safe. My father did not, either. He was a social worker who sometimes visited clients in the countryside. From time to time, he took all of us along for the ride. Late one night, driving home, he stopped to give a man a ride. Instead of riding in the back with her three young daughters and seating the stranger up front with my father,

---

I am not fit to be her mother.

---

she took my brother with her in the front. To make room to fit, the stranger held me on his lap, and soon I felt him stroking my genitals, again and again. I was horrified, terrified. Why didn't she care enough to at least keep me safe?

My father, Emmanuel, was my hero because he was intelligent and funny, and because he cooked, he cleaned and he cared for my mother during her constant psychosomatic illnesses. He constantly encouraged us to do more with our lives than he had, just as he had accomplished more than his father. But he was a monster, too. Some nights, he would pull a big empty hemp rice bag down over one of us, throw the chosen victim over his shoulder and run up and down the corridor, shouting that he would feed us to the bogeyman who lived in the huge tree in the backyard. We would scream and scream in stark terror. One night I watched him do it to one of my sisters. I noticed him chuckling, saw the look of pleasure on his face and realized he was a sadist. My mother never stopped him.

Known as Kazi to his friends and relatives, my father studied Hindu philosophy and taught us that we had chosen Edith and him to be our parents, that we had each created a blueprint of our life experiences, all of which we had chosen. Yet he beat us unmercifully, usually because my mother had complained. He threatened to disfigure us, so no one would ever look at us, if we ran away from home. I still carry scars from his beatings.

When I was fourteen, my seventeen-year-old sister eloped. Bitter and betrayed, my father wrote the rest of us an eight-page letter—both back and front—that told us he no longer cared about us. I had been abandoned again. From then on, when he beat me I felt no fear, no hate, no anger, only the physical pain. I became emotionally numb. My mother meant no more to me than a piece of furniture. I married the man she picked for me, but I didn't love him. He was emigrating to Canada—he was my escape from my home, my ticket to freedom.

When our daughter, Meera, was born, I was determined to be a better mother than Edith had been. I read every parenting book I could get my hands on. My husband called me a "book mama."

She would be better off living with her father.

Meera was hugged and fed and protected and deeply loved. I was so fiercely protective of her I hardly even let other people hug her, lest she pick up a germ.

I left my husband and took Meera with me when she was five and a half. I wanted a career, and he wanted a homemaker. During those six months alone with my daughter, I could see that Meera missed her father very much and was unhappy. She accused me of not loving her. This was painful and pivotal. When my daughter said that, I slowly realized my greatest fear: I was becoming as dysfunctional and as disconnected as Edith had been. And now, I had put my daughter in danger. I was neglecting her, even abusing her. She would be better off living with her father.

The only way I could protect Meera from myself was to give her up. When I told her we were going to live away from him she had asked me: "Is Daddy going to be okay?"

I explained to her the wonderful things about the new location, and she was young enough to see it as an adventure. Six months later, I told her: "You are going to live with your Dad for a while." She was happy packing, happy the day she left. It ripped my heart out, and I felt like a failure. However, it was most important to me that she was happy, and she WAS happy.

I didn't see her for six whole months while I combated my feelings of failure and heartache by submerging myself in weekly counseling. I had to work hard to open myself up to feeling again to become the mother I wanted to be, and so I wouldn't be like my parents. It took time.

My healing was not only psychological, but deeply spiritual. To rid myself of the limiting beliefs my parents had engrained in me, I cut off contact with them for eight years. In fact, for a while during that time, my father was at the same university as I was, and I would walk past him without saying a word.

When Meera was younger, I definitely didn't want her to visit my parents when she first moved in with her father, but he would take her there anyway. And he would leave her there! I blew my top every time I found out.

After many years, I was able to really forgive myself. And once I was able to do that, I could forgive my parents and express my gratitude for their chosen role in my life. I've broadened my education and developed relationships with my siblings. But best of all, I've established a wonderful relationship with my daughter.

That took some doing. Meera lived with me during her early teens then moved back with her father to finish high school. She returned to me when she was accepted at the University of Toronto, as I lived closer to the university.

Because she felt I'd abandoned her when I sent her to live with her father, and because the guilt of that abandonment haunted me, Meera and I had an uneasy relationship during her teen years. But one day my sister, Rheah, asked her, "Do you want to have the kind of relationship that your mother has with *her* mother?"

Even my cousin, Meela, encouragingly told Meera: "Your mother takes every course, every seminar, every opportunity for healing, all in hope of healing her relationship with you. Do you want to continue this way and have the relationship Jeunesse has with Edith, or do you want to try to work through your issues?"

We did have that talk, the first of so many. It was as though a cloud burst, my head cleared, and I found my reason for living again: a fresh start with my daughter. We were making our way back, as from the ashes of a burned house. I took her with me to the many self-help and spiritual workshops I attended; this was one of my bridges to building a relationship with her. Finally, Meera

---

I was able to break the chain forever and create a new legacy with Meera, one of respect, love and harmony.

---

understood that I had protected her as best I could, protected her from the unhappy, dysfunctional person I was when she was little; and I finally accepted that my decision to give her up hadn't made me a horrible person. I shudder to think what may have happened if I *hadn't* made that choice.

Meera understood that I had spent the next decade—and more—on a quest to become the person who would be worthy to be her mother. That quest helped me realize that my father was right, we do choose our experiences, and that those experiences mold us, depending upon how we perceive them. We all know that there are plateaus, dips and bends in the road of life. Our joy and happiness depend on how we travel that road. It means the world to me that Meera now calls me her best friend.

Abuse and neglect were passed down to me along with my brown eyes and brown skin. But I refused to continue that legacy with my own daughter, even if it meant letting her go. And in giving her up, I was able to break the chain forever and create a *new* legacy *with* Meera, one of respect, love and harmony.

Being your Daughter
by Meera Boodhoo
May 10, 2009

You are my closest friend.
I have learned from your experiences.
I continue to learn from you.
You taught me without me knowing.
Being your daughter

Jeunesse Hosein, BA, JD, is passionate about helping people remove the veils that prevent them from seeing their true selves and their inner light. As a practitioner of psychosomatic therapy and a life coach, she has helped many people shed their limiting beliefs so that they can manifest their desires. She teaches people how to connect with the circles of light that exist around our bodies. After working as a provincial and municipal prosecutor for eighteen years, she now has her own law practice, which has allowed her to expand and share her spiritual awareness. Connect with Jeunesse at www.JeunesseHosein.com.

Sonia Azizian

Coming Out

*I*t was unreal. I couldn't believe after all those years, after everything I had learned in order to love, accept and find the courage to express myself in my own, authentic way, I was living a secret life—again. I was back in the closet.

Inside I was suffering, living in fear of what my family would think. How would they see me? Would they take me seriously and judge me? Would they dismiss the last decade of my life as just a gay "phase?" Would they accept me as a bisexual woman? I felt like a ton of bricks was lying heavy on my chest, my heart stifled and afraid to fall in love for fear of being judged by my family and friends.

I had identified as a lesbian for well over a decade and was even married to a woman for five years. After she and I split, I found myself attracted to a man for the first time in ages, a good friend I'd met in a personal growth class. We started a long-distance relationship that made it easy for me to hide, lie and keep him a secret from my family and friends—especially my gay friends.

I'd already been treated as a deviant by straight society. Was I going to be judged that way by "my gays," too? Gay men and lesbians consider bisexuals the "deviants" of the gay community—confused, in denial or selfish cowards unwilling to take a real risk. I couldn't even say the *word* "bisexual" out loud because I *was* in denial and feared being judged. For two years I was beginning a downward spiral of depression, suffering from lying to everyone I loved about who I really was—and, more importantly, lying to myself.

No box was ever the right size for me to fit into. As a biracial child, half Filipino and half Armenian, I felt like an outcast in both cultures. I started kindergarten in California the year my parents divorced and finished in the Philippines. I was baptized twice—once as an Armenian Apostolic Christian and a second time as a Filipino Roman Catholic. Confusion and searching for connection just became part of who I was.

Would they accept me as a bisexual woman?

I felt I could never even be accepted as biracial within my own family. During weekend visits with my dad, he'd often ask, "Do you tell your friends you're Armenian or Filipino?"

To which I would answer, "I tell them that I'm *both,* Dad." In high school, I was the neighborhood gangster and a role model. The popular girl and the bully. A drug-user and a straight-A student. A truant involved with student government. A tomboy and a girly-girl. I both loved and hated everyone. I was *totally* "bi."

The Webster's definition of "bi" is "two," "twice," doubly" and "on both sides." I've always been bi—in every way I have been *both.* But perhaps most notably, I am bisexual. It just took many years for me to realize it, and I definitely couldn't admit it until recently.

Coming out the first time was hard enough. Being gay was never an option for me growing up. I was Catholic, and it was against God's rules—I would go to hell if I were gay. It wasn't until I was in my late twenties that I fell in love with Nina and realized: "This is what I've been looking for my whole life."

Coming out to my mom was easy because she's compassionate and forgiving. Telling my dad didn't go as well; he raged and screamed. But coming out to my grandma was the hardest thing I'd ever done in my life.

My grandmother, Mercedes, was tough as nails, the matriarch of my family, and I was her eldest grandchild—expected to be at her beck and call. So as a kid, I became her shadow. And after Nina and I got together, I took care of my grandma until she died. I thought she must have known Nina was my girlfriend—we were together all the time. Finally, on her deathbed, I got up the courage to tell her.

"Grandma," I said, crying, "Nina is my girlfriend, you know, like my wife." There was a long, uncomfortable silence. She just glared at me. *What are you thinking, Grandma?* I felt like I might pass out, but instead I continued, "Are you okay? Grandma, is that okay with you?"

"Is that *okay?*" she snapped. "Of course it's okay! If it wasn't, then that would make me ignorant." She was pissed at me for underestimating her! I cried tears of joy and relief, feeling the heavy weight I'd been carrying on my back and in my chest instantly

---

*No box was ever the right
size for me to fit into.*

---

dissipate and disappear. I could finally breathe. If Grandma knew and had accepted me, I didn't really care about what anyone else in the family thought, even after my dad pounded his fist on the hood of his car and cried out, "What have I done? I should have never left!" My grandma had accepted me, and that was just enough.

After Nina and I split up, I met Michelle. Though it wasn't legal, we married in San Francisco, exchanged rings and planned wholeheartedly to be together forever. By then I had become accustomed to rising to the challenge of coming out to absolutely everyone who wanted to know about my background: new friends, clients, colleagues. "Yes, I'm married, but I don't have a husband. My wife's name is Michelle." I no longer hid my sexuality from anyone. I lived with pride.

Five years later, our divorce and the economy's effect on my industry—real estate—hit me hard, but it was denying my sexuality once I started dating both men and women that made me feel depressed. I stopped doing personal growth work and taking care of myself. I didn't realize that, since the divorce, I had filled my life with so much busy work that I wouldn't have to address the "BI" issue. I just skated along, avoiding the conversation except with the few I would date. Even then, I always had to defend myself when women would ask me, "How do you know you want to be with women?" Or when men would ask, "How do you know you want to be with men?"

I began to focus more on my Buddhist practice and chanted for the wisdom to understand my life. Nichiren Buddhism encourages us to look inside and reveal our true identities as enlightened leaders for change and world peace. So I chanted to reveal my true nature and took more personal growth classes. Looking

I have to keep it real: This is who I am.

deeper into myself, I came to the realization that by denying my bisexuality, I was denying a fundamental part of myself and that I could never be absolutely happy living a life that was suppressed. I knew I couldn't bounce back from my depression until I stopped hiding and lived an honest, authentic life once more.

In October 2010, I came out for the second time in my life as a bisexual woman. I am not confused. This is an important part of who I am. I am capable of loving both men and women because it's the heart connection that matters most.

It was tough coming out again. I lost friends in the lesbian community, women I thought would always be on my side. Most of my family and straight friends just shrugged their shoulders and said, "Hey, it's all good." No big deal.

And when I told my mom she sighed with relief. My resolution with my father would come later.

Now, whenever I meet someone new, I have to clarify. *Here we go again…* "No, it wasn't my ex-husband, it was my ex-*wife*." I have to come out every time. They might question, judge or frown, but it's my truth. And though Grandma is gone, I know she would approve.

I have to keep it real: This is who I am. I am never going to fit into any one box, nor would I want to. I'm never going to be the perfect little housewife, the good Catholic girl or the poster child for lesbianism. I'm straddling many different worlds: I'm bisexual, biracial, a Buddhist within two Christian families and a seeker who was not born to "fit in" anywhere. I am a dynamic, whole, valuable woman capable of anything I choose to commit myself to. I can have and be all that I am. I am a leader for change and world peace. Embracing all aspects of myself allows me to love others more completely. And being accepted by others isn't as essential as being accepting of myself.

Other opinions of me are not as important as my opinion of myself, and following my heart is what's most important. I now live my life by the Buddhist concept of *hon nim myo,* which means, "from this moment on." I know I can never change the past and the pain of living a secret life. But I can always strive to be true to myself and to do my best in every new moment, and the next, and the next.

All of us have secrets. All of us have truths about ourselves that we may be afraid to share, but when we do, it allows us to become more of who we're meant to be. I have done my soul-searching as an Armenian, Filipino, twice-baptized-raised-Christian-and-Catholic child, lesbian and bisexual Buddhist. I now understand that my journey is not about a journey of confusion, it's been a journey of self-discovery. I have discovered my multi-faceted, authentic self. And I love it!

When I came out as bisexual to my dad, we were at the zoo where he used to take me as a little girl. I was nervous again to tell him, afraid that like the first time, he would be outraged, angry and heartbroken. I said, "Dad, why don't you ever ask me about my relationships?"

He replied, "I know that you've had one or two girlfriends before, and I've learned to accept that."

I wasn't convinced that he had truly accepted it, and that thought made me a little sad. Then I told him, "I want you to know that since Michelle and I split up, I've dated a couple of guys and… I'm bisexual." This time, he perked up, looked at me with total excitement and hugged and kissed me on the cheek.

I was so relieved! I said, "I was afraid to tell you, Dad, because I didn't want to disappoint you and break your heart again."

He said, "It's okay. All I want is for you to be happy." I know now that whomever I choose to love in the future, male or female, he'll be okay. And now that I continue to speak my truth, I'll be okay, too. We all will.

Sonia Azizian earned her bachelor's degree in economics with a specialization in Asian-American studies from UCLA. A successful entrepreneur with several companies since 1994, Sonia has applied coaching techniques to assist her business clients in achieving their goals. As an effective and compassionate MMS life coach and speaker, Sonia motivates others to accept and love themselves completely. She is currently completing her next book, BEing BIsexual—How to Love From the Heart, *to be released in 2012.*

Sonia has a passion for people, culture and nature that has inspired her to travel the world photographing life's incredible scenes. She has an innate desire to continue her own personal growth and education using the world as her teacher and classroom. Connect with Sonia at www.CreateYourWay. com.

Celest Turner

Butterfly

Heart thumping a mile a minute, panting with anxiety, I turn away from the ballroom of the Lord Baltimore Hotel and half-walk, half-run across its rich burgundy carpets and cool marble floors to the large, beveled front doors. *I have to get out of here.*

My corporate colleagues are all still in the ballroom, hundreds of them, assembled in tight cliques; these are people I have been working with for months, but we only say hi and goodbye. Most of them probably don't even know my name.

I'm in my last year of college, and I landed my first corporate job before I graduated. Excited? I am way beyond that. I don't need an alarm clock to wake up in the mornings. I just leap up like a Pop-Tart® from a toaster. I want to be the best I can possibly be and get ahead, so I get to work early and leave late, work hard and try to learn everything I can. I do my full eight hours—no smoke breaks, no chats at the water cooler, no friends to gossip with. Just nose down in work.

I couldn't wait to get here for my first big company meeting today. To the twenty-three-year-old me, the hotel looked like something out of a fairy tale. A bellman greeted me as I walked in the front doors, and an antique, burnished-wood easel pointed me to the ballroom. The sound of my heels clicking down the marble hallway thrilled me. I quietly found my way through the crowd to the front of the room to hear the company execs speak. They showed their fancy slides, got us pumped and we were through.

Oh, crap—time to mingle. Instantly, I felt mortified. Paralyzed. My breath quickened. I heard my heart beat and actually put my hand to my chest to see if it was beating as hard as it sounded. I wore an awkward half-smile as my eyes tried desperately to fix on one person whom I could hide with, but as I scanned the room, I saw nothing but cliques.

The Marketing Girls: Twenty- and thirty-somethings smiling, chatting, laughing and sipping on drinks. They look like they're actually having fun;

And then there's me—as invisible and out of place as the kid in school whom both the cool kids and the glee club think is weird.

The Customer Service Crew: Entry-level folks, mostly older and African-American, laughing gregariously and bonding over the common impossibilities of their jobs;

The Golden Boys: Thirty-plus-year-old white guys in crisp white shirts and starched khakis, all VPs or in sales;

The Butterflies: The very small, mysterious group of people who float easily between groups;

And of course *The Nosers,* hovering near the execs to try and strike up a conversation given the least smidgen of opportunity.

And then there's me —as invisible and out of place as the kid in school whom both the cool kids and the glee club think is weird.

As I stood there paralyzed, the room started to blur. I couldn't see individual faces anymore, just groups, and I couldn't hear the conversations around me anymore either—just loud buzzing sounds. *Soon they'll all see how socially inept I am. I'd better make a run for it.* And that's when I fled the ballroom, my breathing easier with every inch I put between me and the faceless groups of people still milling around behind me.

I remember exactly when all this started: I was in preschool near my grandparents' row house in Baltimore. After school each day I played with my cousin, who was a little older than me. When we sat on the steps and played jacks or hopscotch, just the two of us, everything was fine. I was just Little Desie (I have no clue how they got that nickname from Celestine). But when the other older neighborhood girls showed up, things changed. When the group formed, I got picked on.

One day a big bunch of these girls, who were all two- to five-years older than I was, gathered to jump rope and play double dutch. As they played, they shot me smirking looks and sang the theme song to the cartoon *Josie and the Pussycats*. Now, my

---

People were scary because they changed in groups—especially if they wanted to fit in.

---

mother's name is Josephine, and she went by Josie, so this was an obvious attack. "Stop singing that song," I called out. My cousin had joined the group and was now singing along. "Stop it!"

The girls formed a circle around me. There was the face of my cousin, a face I thought I knew, twisted into an ugly mask and laughing. "Josie and the *Pussy*cats! Josie and the *Pussy*cats!"

"Shut up!" I yelled, as my face grew puffy with anger. "STOP!" But the more upset I got, the more they taunted me. Episodes like that occurred repeatedly throughout my childhood. I learned that social situations were not a safe place. People were scary because they changed in groups—especially if they wanted to fit in.

I was always a quiet little girl, a high achiever and a bookworm. My family and kids called me "Tweety Bird" because of my big head, short hair and the glasses I wore since I was tiny. I never learned the social skills other girls learned through playing together; I was in my own little world most of the time. And it got worse as I got older and the taunting continued. Sometimes I surprised everyone by suddenly snapping and fighting back, hitting or punching until the teasing stopped. But mostly I just tried to stay invisible.

So, a natural introvert, I became shy on top of it. Although I loved being with people one-on-one and had a few good friends, I was terrified of whom they could become in groups and avoided at all costs social situations with too many unknowns. In college, I went from class to my room, class to my room, and barely even looked at anyone until Nyya, a hip and popular girl from Brooklyn, caught me near the elevator in the hall one day and said, "Hey, how come you never talk to anyone?" She wasn't being mean, just curious.

I looked at her, a little puzzled—she had broken through my bubble. "I don't know," I said. It was true. I had never really thought about it.

A few years later, in my new and exciting corporate job, I went into my boss's office for my six-month review. I felt so confident in my work that I half-listened to her, waiting for the words, "exceeds expectations." Everything before that sounded like the adults from the *Charlie Brown* cartoon. And then she said, "Celest, you're

---

But what my boss was saying to me was that
my fear was stopping me from growing.

---

doing a great job. But to move up, people need to know who you are. The right people don't know what you can do." I was shocked. I thought that I could always get by on my achievements alone. But what my boss was saying to me was that my fear was stopping me from growing.

Over the next couple of months, I kept turning her words over in my head. I wanted to move ahead. I didn't want to be handicapped by my social anxiety. So I started literally forcing myself to talk to other people, shoving myself toward strangers in other cubes and asking how their weekends were, or approaching coworkers in the break room. "Oh, how's the coffee today?" It felt clumsy and anxious, but I kept trying.

Then came the big company event, and the true test. Could I move forward with my life? Or would I always hold myself back?

As I stood at the front door of the hotel, about to push through and find relief by fleeing for good, I paused. I heard a voice: *If you want to move up, you're going to have to do this.* And an argument ensued in my head, *Just leave. It's okay. You'll meet these people eventually.* Another voice said, *But this is the perfect opportunity, Celest. Get back in there!* I closed my eyes and breathed deeply. *Okay. You can do this. You can do this.* I opened my eyes, turned around and slowly walked back toward the ballroom.

Shaking, I walked up to the bar and ordered a soda to buy a moment and have something to hold. Then I looked again at the group of lively marketing ladies, laughing and having a good time.

My baggage, my old identity and fear, had felt safe, but it was a barrier to my growth and success.

I swallowed. *Okay. One. Two. Three. Go!* I shot forward through the crowd, my hand outstretched, and blurted rapidly, "Hi, I'm Celest, I'm in customer retention and I'm in school."

A smiling woman reached out her hand to take mine. "I'm Kim," she said. "So nice to meet you!" And just like that, she built a bridge.

The conversation wasn't easy for me—I was so nervous I either babbled or fell into awkward silences. But having the courage to walk up to the marketing ladies changed my perspective enough for me to start turning my whole life around. It gave me back a little of the confidence I lost so long ago as others scratched at me in their own desperate efforts to belong, and I started to push past the don't-hurt-me wall that held me back. My baggage, my old identity and fear, had felt safe, but it was a barrier to my growth and success. I realized that people weren't so scary. I started to see my life through adult eyes.

Just a few months later, Kim recommended me to her boss for a position on the marketing team, and I was promoted just nine months after I started with the company.

My life completely changed because I decided to take a risk. I now know how that Sally Field Oscar-like moment of "You like me! You really like me!" feels. And now I can experience the joy that comes because I finally gave myself permission to leave my cocoon and become the butterfly that I was always meant to be.

Celest Turner, a masterful success coach and transformational speaker, has perfected strategies that have developed leaders, enhanced lives and increased revenue for companies. Celest's experience with large enterprises, small businesses and ambitious individuals has led her to develop a unique process for creating a holistic success roadmap that helps people and businesses achieve goals and improve their perception of their own success. Celest is available for coaching, training and speaking engagements. Learn more about her by visiting www.GrowthByCelest.com or follow her on Twitter at growthbycelest.

Sharon C. Evans

Holding My Life's Work in My Hands

I have to finish this. I have to! I looked around the hotel room I'd checked into for the weekend in sheer desperation. Innumerable piles of paper were stacked on both beds and the table and spread across the carpet. I'd arrived on Friday afternoon, and it was now late Saturday night. I'd hardly eaten or slept. Had I even brushed my teeth? *I am in DEEP.*

I'd been working on my book for over a year, and the pressure to finish it had been mounting steadily since my book-coach deadline of one hundred and eighty days passed me by months before. Since then I'd felt my already-compromised immune system totally breaking down from stress. The smaller my world got—the book, work, the book, work, the book, the book, the book—the more exhausted I became. Would I ever finish?

The book was my biggest dream so far. It meant the world to me to prove to myself that I could do it. But the project had come to dwarf everything else, and now burdened my home life to the breaking point. I was afraid that if I didn't finish it soon, my husband Ron would never let me have another chance. He was sick and tired of hearing me talk about the book; he just wanted his wife, the mother of his child, back.

Ron had spent extra time with our toddler, Derek, to give me space. But there was no place in the house where I could focus completely, so I checked into the hotel with a giant file-carrier and a cardboard box full of my materials. At first I was so pumped up—it seemed like a mini-vacation. But I always overestimated what I could do, and when I checked in I actually thought, *I could complete this book in a weekend!*

In the wee hours of the morning, heading into Sunday, I knew: *There was no way that is going to happen.* I had a sick, plummeting feeling in my stomach, as if I'd lost sight of my son in a playground.

Would I ever finish?

And by the time I checked out on Sunday afternoon, I knew I was just looking at the base of a mountain. But I had to see it through—I had to prove to myself that I could do it, no matter the cost.

Becoming an author was my lifelong dream. I started writing little books at about age seven: *My First Musical. How to Create the Best Science Fair Project Ever.* The science fair booklet was my first, and I wrote it after winning the first fair I ever entered with my project on Wales. The moment my prize was announced, I jumped up and down. My first thought was, "I *won!* I should write a book about this!"

So I wrote my little book on foolscap, and proudly put it in a binder to show my family and friends. I even took it to show-and-tell at school. My cover art was beautiful—a picture of the Welsh countryside. In the background were deep valleys dotted with leek blossoms, the Welsh national flower. Everyone was so impressed. When I heard, "Excellent writing, Sharon!" and "Very good!" I beamed with pride. The positive feedback was addictive. I loved being able to hold what I had created in my own two hands and say, "Look what I did!" From then on, every time I faced a challenge and overcame it, I wrote another small book.

When I grew up, I became a successful enterprise architect and international consultant. And I kept writing—mostly architecture blogs and newsletters. My work was the epitome of the technical, and I noticed that no one ever talked about the personal aspects of the work, or what it took to be really good at it. One day, I had an epiphany. *The most critical skill for this job is being able to see the big picture AND all the minute details.* I thought of it as "The Zoom Factor": the ability to zoom in to look at the details and then zoom out, when needed, to look at the whole scope of a project.

Excited and inspired, I asked myself, *I wonder if I could teach people this skill?* The idea for my real book—my life's work—was born.

When I first spoke on the subject, people rushed the stage when I was finished—the response was overwhelming. I felt as proud and special as I had when I'd presented my first book at show-and-tell. *So this* can *be a book! I have a lot of work ahead of me.* But there were some important details complicating the process that I forgot to zoom in and examine closely.

For one, I was a mom, and I already struggled with my guilt over not having enough time with Derek or my husband. I worked full-time as a consultant during the day while coaching fellow

---

*I was to write the whole book in just
one hundred and eighty days.*

---

enterprise architects in the evenings. And I had been battling an auto-immune condition for years. Thanks to medication, it was under control and had been for well over a decade. But the balance was already so tenuous, I worried. *If I add one more big commitment, the stress might make me really sick. Try to cram a book into* this *life?*

I hired a book coach to help me create the book, but after laying out thousands of dollars, the process of writing it looked more complicated than ever. Trying to follow their complicated programs and what seemed like insane deadlines started to make me panic. Still, as I listened to hours of audio recordings and flipped through their materials, I thought, *If I just follow their system, I can't go wrong.* I was to write the whole book in just one hundred and eighty days.

I was on a consulting site every day, and at lunch I skipped taking a walk or eating to work on my book instead, dictating into an audio recorder. After work, I picked up Derek from daycare, and continued writing late at night after I'd put him to bed and done my evening coaching sessions. During the week I'd set my alarm for five o'clock to have an extra hour to write in the mornings. "Just one more hour," I begged Ron. I was running myself ragged. But I was determined to write my book in the allotted time.

My February weekend in the hotel led to almost seven more months of this crazy schedule. By September, I had finished writing my book, and knew I needed to hire an editor to help me cut it down drastically. But I was also full-blown ill—as I had feared. In the past, I had needed an intervention of a super-steroid about once a year to keep me in good shape. By mid-October, I needed one every five days. The more I worked, the worse I felt; but I couldn't stop. One day, my mother came to visit. She took one look at me, at the dark circles under my dull eyes, my colorless face, and made me sit down in a chair. "You've got to slow down and take care of yourself," she said.

"I know, I know", I said. After she left, I burst into tears.

Ron was irritated at my lack of progress, and I was so worried I was going to lose him. I had promised him so many times, "I'm almost finished!"

"I've heard this before, Sharon," he said. "I'm just about done."

"But this is so important to me, Ron. I just need a little more time!" He would shrug and walk away. I felt so disconnected from him, so alone. It felt like he didn't see or hear me anymore.

He wanted me to better balance work and family life, and also to admit my dream was not realistic. I'd talked about so many lofty goals, and he was now skeptical that the book would ever get completed. His body language no longer welcomed me. It said, "Why can't you just wrap this project up, pay more attention to us?" The sadness of that hung heavy on my soul.

Ron kept saying, "You've got to think about what you can eliminate from your schedule." I was extremely fatigued, and had to make sure I stretched often and didn't sit typing too long. My editor and I had a schedule, but I kept missing deadlines and still felt the same urgency. My head was so muddled by exhaustion I didn't think the material I was giving the editor was good enough. In retrospect, I should have just handed it over to her and trusted.

So many times, I just felt like giving up. But as I kept explaining to Ron what it would mean to me to have this book to hold in my hands that was full of everything I believed in, and how creating this resource could ultimately improve the quality of life for all of us in the long-run, I knew I had to see it through.

Then one night, Derek ran into the office just after I'd closed myself in to work, wanting to curl up in my arms and watch a

---

I knew I had to see it through.

---

movie about sharks. With wrenching guilt, I thought, *am I letting my life pass me by?* I picked him up after watching the video, took him back to Ron and said, "Can you just try to entertain him? I really need to finish this."

Ron said, "You always say that. I'm telling you—you just gotta finish it. This can't go on." What could I do to make this final process go faster? The stress of knowing how important it was for me to just finish—and yet wishing I could spend all night with my son—was devastating.

Carving out a few minutes here and there to put my life's work into writing might make it a slow process, but at least I'd be around, with Derek and Ron, to enjoy the fruits of my labors. *I need to get focused.* I started laying down some serious strategy, and coming up with the hooks in my book. Then I let my editor do her magic. When I let go, and began to eat and sleep regularly again, it was no surprise to me that my health was on the rebound in almost no time. I went off the steroids, and have not needed them since.

In my journey to completing my life's work, I had forgotten to take all of my own advice. I had lost sight of the very core technique I'd been writing about for months in blind pursuit of my own goal:

keeping track of the big picture while working through detail and constantly readjusting, refocusing and evaluating. I learned a tough lesson, which I knew I'd never forget—but I did make my big dream come true. And now I knew I had it in me, ideas for books started coming so quickly I thought my head might explode.

A couple of days before Christmas, two "pilot" copies of my book arrived from the publisher. I sat on the floor of my office while Ron held Derek so I could rip open the package with shaking hands. My book! I turned it over in my hands—it was beautiful. The cover illustration looked even better, sharper than the images I'd been shown online. I opened to the dedication page, where I knew I would read: "To Derek." I couldn't believe it. After more than thirty years of wanting to write a real book, I'd finally done it.

Ron looked at me in awe. "That's awesome," he said. "Look, Derek, Mommy did it!" I put my head down and started to cry in relief. *He finally believes in me!* I took Derek on my knee. *I don't need anything more than this.*

"What's wrong, Mommy?" Derek asked, surprised.

"Mommy is just so happy that I had to cry," I said, smiling through my tears. "Sometimes big people are just so happy they can't believe it, so they cry. But don't worry. I'm very happy. Very, very, very happy." Christmas had come, two days early.

Sharon C. Evans trains and coaches people to find their "Zoom Factor" and use the principles of productivity and strategic planning and easy Internet tools to achieve their entrepreneurial vision. After writing her first book, Zoom Factor for the Enterprise Architect, *Sharon became an expert at creating products quickly via teleseminars, eBooks and video. Her second book,* Zoom Factor for the Business Owner: How to Bring Laser Focus to Your Efforts and Boost Your Productivity, *is forthcoming. Read Sharon's blog and learn about her workshops, online courses, group seminars and finding your own Zoom Factor at www.SharonCEvans.com.*

Karen Underwood

Living on My Own Terms

There was nothing I could do. The prayer I said over and over and over during the beatings—*Dear God, please make him stop*—still didn't help. My raging father had thrown me to the floor and was standing over me, one foot on either side of my body like a menacing human tower, kicking and slapping me with that familiar, cruel scowl on his face. His tongue protruded from his mouth, as if he couldn't even contain his desire to hurt me. "You are not welcome in my house anymore," he snarled. "Disappear."

I had gone to see my boyfriend, Chuck, and now I was being punished for it. I wept with fear and shame as I lay curled in a fetal position for protection, my body aching, my ears ringing, the taste of blood in my mouth. At nineteen, I was so terrified I had peed my favorite nightgown—the one with the little pink flowers and cotton eyelet collar that my grandmother had so lovingly made for me.

My mother once told me that, just after I was born and she was being wheeled out of the delivery room, my parents consoled each other by saying, "Don't worry, next time we'll have a boy." From the beginning, I was not what was hoped for. Instead, I became the repository for my ex-Marine father's rage. My younger brother, Kit, was always the pride and joy. I deeply loved my mother, but aside from one occasion, which earned her a hard slap in the face, she never stepped in to help me, and I was left alone after the beatings to comfort myself. Kit tried once to defend me and was slapped so hard he flipped right out of his chair. After that, they never chimed in to protect me. They were too afraid.

As soon as school was over, I would run home while my father was still at work, change into my play clothes and play outside until dark, building forts and tree houses, safe places and alternate homes where I wouldn't have to gauge the emotional temperature.

"You are not welcome in my house anymore," he snarled. "Disappear."

At home, I had to be hyper-vigilant. If I walked in the door and smelled cigarette smoke, I knew he was there; if not, I knew I was safe for a little while.

When I got older, I noticed the ads for Breck shampoo on the back cover of *LIFE* magazine. They showed a beautiful girl, usually blonde, with hair so perfect you could see the comb marks. One evening, I arranged my hair like the Breck girl, put on a dab of the "Evening in Paris" perfume my grandmother had given me and came proudly downstairs to set the table. My father looked up and said, "You smell like a whore."

Chuck and I fell in love when we were both eighteen. He lived in New York and I lived outside of Boston, so we talked on the phone and wrote letters. My father always answered the phone, in case it was a boy; if it was, I had three minutes to talk, with him standing in the room. When he knew I was getting letters from Chuck, he stole them.

I had a job at a nursery, and my father drove me to and from work every day. The owners, the Melgrins, knew that I was like a prisoner at home, so they let me talk to Chuck on the phone at their house, and he and I made secret plans for him to come and visit me. He came to the nursery on a motorcycle, covered in black leather so that even if my father saw him he wouldn't know who he was. We had the most wonderful picnic by the lake in the sunshine, eating food that the Melgrins had made for us. They were what my family *should* have been.

One day, Chuck called from New York and said he really needed to see me. Could I come and meet him in Boston? "If you leave this house," my father said, "you're never setting foot in it again." But as it got dark, I snuck out of the house, took off my shoes and ran through the muddy cornfield between my house and the main street where the bus stopped, so that I'd be hidden if my father noticed I was gone. Then I ran like a bat out of hell down the sidewalk and hid, shaking, until the bus arrived.

I stayed overnight in Boston, but the next day, my mother reached me and said, "Honey, just come home—everything's going to be all right." Though he was terribly nervous about it and really worried for me, Chuck brought me home, and, trembling, I dressed for my afternoon shift at the family business, a glass and

---

They were what my family should *have been.*

---

china shop. My father was there when I arrived, but to my surprise, he didn't hit me. He didn't even look at me strangely. I couldn't believe it. At the end of the workday, he even decided we'd go out for dinner.

I sat there with my stomach churning, waiting for something terrible to happen, but dinner was actually pleasant. When we came home, I ran up the stairs to get ready for bed and put on my favorite nightgown. That was when my mother called, from the foot of the stairs, "Honey, you need to come down here," and I walked into the family room to find my father there, waiting for me. *Dear God, please make him stop.* He must have been waiting, all day, to decide how he should hurt me.

A peculiar quiet ensued in the days that followed that last beating, as I prepared to finally leave. I'd found a job as chef for the president of Wesleyan University, and I counted the hours until I reached that refuge. I was so relieved to leave; I felt myself breathe for the first time ever without fear lurking in the corners of my mind. I experienced this joy for several months, but then Thanksgiving came, and I couldn't go home. My mother wrote: "You can come home for Christmas, but you'll have to write your father a letter saying you'll never see Chuck again." As Christmas approached, I wrote the letter. It was a lie; I wanted to *marry* Chuck. I just missed my mother, my grandmother and Kit so badly. It was a fairly nice Christmas; I didn't get hit.

I went back to Connecticut. Two weeks later my mother called and said the words I'd been secretly waiting to hear for years: "Karen, your father had a massive heart attack. He's dead." Her words were flat, matter-of-fact, but I could hear a deep relief in her

---

He must have been waiting, all day, to decide how he should hurt me.

---

voice and felt relief mixed with a bit of grief flow into me instantly. I was beyond grateful—my body felt lighter, freer, as if it knew the beatings were over and safety was finally possible.

To my dismay, the feeling wouldn't last.

I did marry Chuck, and we had a much-wanted son together. But I found myself struggling with depression. I started seeing a therapist and asked Chuck to go with me. "Why should I go?' he said. "It's your problem, not mine," or, "He was *your* father."

Needing a safe and understanding outlet, I turned to a good friend. I started telling him about my father, the depression, what I was experiencing in therapy and how lonely I felt without Chuck's support. I continued to reach out for Chuck, to hold on to what we initially had, but he was not interested in walking through the fire with me. He was clear that this was not *our* problem; this was *my* problem. Peter was so empathetic and cared so much about me that I started falling in love with him.

Soon after, my relationship with Chuck began to unravel, and neither he nor I cared to make the effort to put it back together. Life gave me a second chance at happiness when I married Peter some years later. We loved each other so much, we could hardly believe our great good fortune. We had a beautiful daughter together; now I was the mother of two cherished children. He started a dream job. Everything felt magical; we had everything.

And then, out of the blue, I began having recurring nightmares. Sometimes there was just a dark, ominous presence in my dreams that I felt was my father. In others, tidal waves approached, about to crash down on me, or I'd struggle against winds so forceful I could barely walk as a bear came to catch me. I'd jerk awake

---

I thought that the fight for my life ended when my dad died, but I was very wrong.

---

in terror, shivering in the dark, then turn to Peter for comfort. He held me tight, and I felt protected for the moment. But the nightmares wouldn't stop, and I began, once again, to slide into a deep depression. I thought that the fight for my life ended when my dad died, but I was very wrong.

I sought help from another therapist, taking time to acknowledge and understand the terrified little girl within. I spent many long hours sobbing uncontrollably, begging for relief: *Lord, please don't make me live with these demons in my head. My father is dead—let me get on with my life!* I worked really hard to push past my anger and send a blessing to the pathetic man who was my dad. I wrote a letter to him, forgiving him for the bruising and belittling of my body and soul. Eventually I began to truly heal, and with the help of medication, I addressed the chemical imbalance that had contributed to my depression. I no longer felt like every movement was as though I was walking through chest-deep water. I could finally breathe again!

Today, I feel blessed to be able to help other women deal with similar issues; I no longer shake or become breathless when I tell some of my stories. I had already lived on my father's terms—now I could live life on my *own* terms, standing in my power. Because of my father I learned three great things: I learned NOT to hate, to forgive and to strive courageously even when feeling the most afraid. I promised myself to raise my children differently, leaving the family trail of my father's abuse in the dust. In loving my children unconditionally, I have breathed life into a new family legacy.

Rising from the most shattering of beginnings, I'm now able to walk life's road, knowing that I can finally create my dream of a life worth living.

Having overcome childhood abuse and major depression, Karen Underwood worked as a national corporate spokeswoman; created a Golden Showcase Award-winning series of videos called "Kids In The Kitchen;" and is a business owner, artist, astrologer and the mother of two wonderful children. After ten years of study with Sri Goswami Kriyananda of The Temple Of Kriya Yoga in Chicago, Illinois, Karen was ordained as Swami Namratananda. She is also trained in crisis counseling as a Stephen's Minister ordained by The Presbyterian Church of Lake Forest, and has worked in trauma intervention for The Trauma Intervention Program (TIP). Karen aspires to teach with warmth, humor, joy and wisdom what she feels has been the greatest blessing to her from combined studies of the spiritual teachings of both East and West. Connect with Karen at www.FeelTheBlessing.com.

Bonnie L. Silver

Pennies from Heaven

Just before Thanksgiving 2008, I finally found my home—a large, pale yellow house in Capistrano Beach California, with ocean views. It had a ton of windows, a gorgeous fireplace and a big open kitchen. It wasn't perfect; it needed TLC; there was trash in the backyard; and it was a vacant short sale. But I felt so pulled to it, I immediately began remodeling in my mind: *I'll knock down this wall and expand the kitchen—then we'll be able to see the ocean from every room in the house.* But what really hooked me were the pennies. I found pennies in every room of the house—I counted seventeen of them.

When I was a little girl, my great-grandmother always gave me pennies. And after she died when I was five, whenever I found a penny, I thought it was her: *Great-grandma's looking after me.* As I grew up, I began to trust that signs and messages were coming to me when I found pennies. People would cross over, and I would find pennies in the most bizarre places with no logical explanation for it. They were pennies from heaven.

I did feel some trepidation about the house. It would be the first I had ever owned by myself. So I had to wonder, *Is this the right decision? Is this really the right house?* When I found all the pennies, I felt sure it was. I was tuned into spirit, and my guardian angels were saying, "This house is for you." As my realtor drew up the paperwork and we submitted the offer, I felt buoyantly confident. *This is our new home!* I couldn't wait to go pick up my six year-old son Keaton from school and give him a huge hug and celebrate our major victory.

The following day, I found a penny in the shower stall. And then I got two text messages from old friends I hadn't spoken to since forever: "Thinking of you and sending you love!" These messages felt like further affirmation, so when the phone rang I jumped with joy and excitement, sure it was the realtor confirming that the owners of my house had accepted my offer.

To my surprise, it was my boss, Mike. Mike was the dream boss: a great listener, totally supportive and always making me feel like an important part of the sales team even though I was telecommuting all the way from the West Coast. Since our

I found pennies in every room of the house—I counted seventeen of them.

relationship always involved a lot of joking and banter, I believed he was kidding when I heard him say, "Bonnie, I am so sorry to inform you that the new owners are letting the outside sales personnel go, and unfortunately, you are one of them." I laughed. "Yeah, right, Mike, that's funny."

"Bonnie, you have been let go. I will do whatever you need, a referral, a recommendation, just let me know." I still didn't get it— Mike had to repeat himself a third time. *Oh my God, really? Is this really happening?* My whole world came crashing down. I was shell-shocked; I truly had not seen this happening.

Nauseous, I started crying. *What do the tears mean? Are they because I just lost the job I love or because I'll miss my boss and co-workers? Are they because I no longer have an income or because my dream of becoming a homeowner is now impossible? I'm a single mom with bills to pay—what am I to do now?*

Blindsided, I let the news sink in for a few hours and then called my realtor. "I lost my job," I told him, trying not to cry.

"I'm so sorry, Bonnie," he said. "You know this voids your contract."

After that call, all I could do was curl up into a ball and cry while Keaton was still at school. At the end of each of my two marriages, I had been the one to move out. Owning my own home had meant so much to me—it meant true independence. I was so

---

God hides his blessings in adversity to surprise us with his love. So something wonderful is around the corner for me.

---

happy to finally do it on my own as a single mom. I felt so fortunate to be making a great living and have it be possible. There was so much to mourn all at once. I was overwhelmed.

As I let myself cry and realize: *as of this moment, there's a whole new plan,* I also thought about the pennies. *Okay, so I misread the signs. They didn't really mean I was going to get the house.* It was my angels telling me, "You know what? Everything's going to be okay. You don't know what's yet to come, but we're here for you."

All those pennies had come just the day before! It couldn't be an accident. This thought helped me let go. *Trust the process,* I thought. Though I was devastated, I had always been a cup half-full kind of person. I did trust that everything happens for a reason. God hides his blessings in adversity to surprise us with his love. So something wonderful is around the corner for me.

I'm going to take this adversity and roll it into one of the best experiences of my life—and I can best do that by serving others. I decided I was going to volunteer everywhere I could for the whole next year. I wanted to give back, and I knew it was the best way to get out of ego and in touch with gratitude. I worked with Talk About Curing Autism (TACA) and the City of Hope Gala; became a Big Sister; and volunteered regularly with my son's class and school. I volunteered in an orphanage in Mexico a few times. Seeing those kids who had nothing, but were so full of light and love, I couldn't help being transformed.

Serving made my heart glow. During this entire year, I searched for a job while collecting unemployment; but I became less concerned with finding a particular kind of job or with what I lacked and just felt grateful for what I did have. My sales career no longer seemed to fit my path, so I broadened my search. And I kept finding pennies. I knew my guides would look after me, whatever happened. I was broke, but I was still tithing ten percent of my unemployment as I continued to trust and have faith in God. I knew I had another calling, and I kept thinking: *I really want to write.* I started researching how to write grants for nonprofits, and I kept journaling.

Writing always came naturally to me; words have always been my gift. I would read the dictionary for fun as a little girl. I loved spelling bees. My mom would always say to me, "Gosh, you write so beautifully." What I couldn't express orally, I could always write

---

I had been working in jobs that earned me a living and not a life. But in my year of service, I was finding my truth.

---

eloquently. But I didn't pursue it because I wasn't in touch with my spirit. I wasn't connected. I was lost. I was in ego. It took a year of service to remember. I had been working in jobs that earned me a living and not a life. But in my year of service, I was finding my truth.

Despite this growth, my finances were in the toilet. The stack of bills was two-feet high. The phone was turned off. My landlord was wonderful and had worked out a deal with me wherein I could fix up and show the house I was living in, which was up for sale. But once I had gone for six months without paying the rent, something had to give.

I asked God, "Okay, what more can I do? I'm putting it all on the line, I'm serving—what more do you want from me? I'm here—use me!" Meditating, I remembered the movie *The Pursuit of Happyness*, and Will Smith's character, who goes to a homeless shelter. And I realized: *My home is inside me. If I'm meant to be homeless, if I'm meant to go to a women's shelter with my son, so be it. It's going to be okay.* Then, I smiled. I thought, *Hmm! I can do that.* I had weathered every other storm and I knew I could survive this one, too.

A moment later, my phone rang. It was my investment company. They had made a series of mistakes with the last of my resources, and I'd given up on ever seeing the money. But on the other end of the line was an agent who said, "We're so sorry for all this trouble. We're wiring this money to your account—we're so sorry."

I just started crying. And I finally turned the corner. I was trying so hard to fix everything. But when I finally said, *Okay, God—we'll be homeless, but we'll have a roof over our heads, my son will appreciate everything that much more, as will I—so be it,* the phone rang and the money appeared.

I surrendered and made that leap within to faith and found that it was for the book in my heart—the song in my soul. I had clarity. I came to realize that I really didn't want another job, and a job wasn't going to bring anything new. Learning to write grants was just skirting the issue. It was a wonderful thing to do, but it wasn't my truth. To write knowing that I had found my calling brought me a sense of completeness, joy and peace. I felt a love for myself that I'd never had before.

First, God taps you on the shoulder. If you don't listen, He shakes you a little. And then He grabs you by both arms and gives you a good shove. I needed the shove. God kept shutting doors so I would open the one door that I was meant to walk through. I reflected: *God didn't give me all these lessons so I could go back to square one—He gave me all these lessons so I could move forward with my dream.*

I had to make the choice to let go of financial security and keep on trusting the process, to believe that everything would indeed be all right, and I was honoring my path by pursuing my gift, the place where I feel most authentic and in tune with my spirit. Once I accepted that, money just came to me.

I realize that the new home that I was willing to pour love into to fix up that started this journey was really just a metaphor for my own soul. I am the house that needed some tender love and care. The serenity that I believed that my new home would bring me needs to live within me, not as an infrastructure. I got the message! I still find pennies everywhere, and when others step over them, I pick them up and know that my great-grandmother is watching over me and smiling.

Bonnie L. Silver, MBA, has lived on each coast of the United States, traveled extensively as a flight attendant and served over six years in the U.S. Army. She is a spiritual intuitive who is dedicated to helping others heal and transform their lives through her writing, healing sessions and workshops, and an author whose forthcoming book, My Life, God's Plan, details her path to transformation and intuitive healing. Connect with Bonnie at www.BonnieLSilver.com.

Kim R. Grimes

Love Gives Second Chances

My husband Lafayette was out on a two-week field training exercise with his Army unit. I had stopped by his commander's house to pick up the dish from the casserole I'd dropped off there for a church function. Somehow, it didn't seem odd that Mike came home wearing his dress blue uniform, or that he'd pulled his wife aside for a hushed conference, or that he skillfully maneuvered me into a sitting position—before gently relating the news that my life was over. My beautiful high school sweetheart and husband of twenty-one months was dead.

As Mike was speaking, I saw his lips moving, but all I could hear was the beating of my heart. Apparently a hunter had mistaken my husband for a deer and shot him. How could that be? How could a man in military uniform, on a field exercise, be mistaken for a deer? How could this happen to me? Killed by a poacher, an illegal hunter during a training mission? The hunter had fled the scene and left my husband to die. Impossible! Twenty-four years old and a widow, how could that be? What did I do so wrong to deserve this? How could something so tragic happen to me? How could God take away the only man that truly loved me for me?

My pain intensified when I realized that I had to call my family and inform Lafayette's mother about what had happened. Mustering up enough strength, I made the dreaded calls; my tear-filled eyes prevented me from clearly seeing the numbers on the phone. I heard the screams and wailing as I delivered the message to first his mother and then my mother. Their grief robbed my body of what little strength I had left. I lost what little control I had; the room went black.

Little did I know that, at the burial, I would lose it all over again. The thought of leaving Lafayette at the cemetery had never entered my mind. Once it did, my screams began to fill the air. I grabbed hold of Lafayette's coffin, clinging on for dear life with both hands.

How could God take away the only man that truly loved me for me?

My oldest brother, Junius, pulled me off. I collapsed in his arms. I awoke in the limo some time later and was amazed to see the seemingly endless procession of cars full of mourners, there to pay their respects to a good, honest, God-loving man.

As the funeral procession moved farther and farther away from the cemetery, putting miles between my love and me, moments— the *best* moments—passed through my mind. Lafayette was responsible for the very best moment of my life. We had just moved to Fort Drum. A new friend of ours, Ja'Donna, took me out shopping on my birthday. When we returned home not a thing was out of place, until a room full of people yelled, "Surprise!"

"Oh, my goodness!" I really couldn't believe it. We had no family there, and not too many friends, and it was just such a great surprise. It touched me because there I was, away from home, away from my family, and even though I had no one there but him, he made me feel comfortable, appreciated and loved, even with the few friends we had made. Still, even this and other treasured memories couldn't shake my heart free from sadness.

After Lafayette's untimely death, I acted out terribly. I drank, smoked and even dated a married man. Hell, I felt if God could take my man, then I could take someone else's. My anger with God propelled me into making poor decisions. I shut God out completely. *How dare He take away the only man I ever loved and who loved me back?* I had reached the lowest low in my life. I had hit bottom. I hated people. I used men. I was seeking vengeance for God taking my man away. I manipulated every man in my life. I saw them as objects, not people. Hurting and in despair, I cussed like a sailor, drank like the town drunk and partied every possible weekend. I ran from the hurt so I couldn't feel the pain, so I could hide from the moments I remembered.

When I met Lionel, my anger and bitterness and alienation from God spilled over into all aspects of my life. *This guy is just another booty call. I'm going to hit and quit it,* I thought. But then something funny happened. Lionel treated me with respect. When

> *I ran from the hurt so I couldn't feel the pain, so I could hide from the moments I remembered.*

I cussed, he'd say, "You're so beautiful, but hearing you use that language messes up the beauty you have." He held up a mirror for me to see how ugly I'd become.

Lionel swore that if God sent him a woman to love, he would love her completely, with all his heart. I'm not sure he bargained for a woman as messed up as I was! I was beyond broken. I was lost. I was angry. I was bitter. I was a pain in the butt! But Lionel didn't judge me; he just found a way to help me see myself in a better light. It was as if with every tender touch, every kind glance he was saying, "Come on now, Kim, you can do this. Come back to life, Kim. I've got you."

One morning I looked and saw my own reflection in the mirror, and for the first time in many moons, I didn't lower my eyes and look away. "This man is an angel straight from God," I said out loud. "God gave me someone who loves me the way Lafayette loved me."

Lafayette. Just his name on my lips caused my heart to swell. I had been pushing him away with drinks and misdeeds for so long,

I couldn't remember the last time I spoke his name and smiled. But with Lionel's love, I felt stronger. So I let the moments come back in. The day we met. The first time he told me he loved me. Our wedding. Every time he made me laugh out loud.

Lionel knew I was still mourning my husband. As I let the moments back in he said, "If you feel like crying, that's okay. I will hold you and if need be I'll cry with you."

That sold me. I was like, "Hot dog! I got me a keeper." That's when I decided, *I'm going to marry this man.*

Lionel had prayed to God to send him a woman to love. When he found me, I was anything but lovable. God sent him someone who needed the unconditional love he could give. I believe God used Lionel to lure me back into His fold. Lionel allowed me to reflect on what kind of woman I wanted to be compared to what

---

To my surprise, I was not alone; my
Heavenly Father was right by my side.

I was. He was more than my angel; he became my champion for integrity, honesty and high moral character. Lionel showed me I was a beautiful woman who deserved love and compassion.

Several years later, I had a dream that Lafayette came to visit me. He didn't say much, just, "I'm fine. Everything will be okay," but it was so wonderful to hear his voice and to see his face. When I awoke I still had unanswered questions. I began to pray to God for answers. I found myself back on the dreadful day, reliving the moments I had pushed away—and kept from myself still, after all these years. I began to see everything that happened to me that day; it was as though I was watching a movie. Mike's dress blues. My washed casserole dish sitting on the counter. The phone in my trembling hand as I relayed the awful news to Lafayette's mother. To my surprise, I was not alone; my Heavenly Father was right by my side.

Feeling I was in the presence of the almighty God, I asked, "Why did this happen to me?" The answer I received was astounding. In the dream God said, "What happened to you was in no way meant to break your spirit, but instead to strengthen it all the more."

I remembered the last moment I saw Lafayette alive. I had come home and laid across the bed, ready for a long rest after dropping him off on-base, when my phone rang. "Baby, I need you to come out to the base. I forgot my dog tags." It was the very last thing I wanted to do, but I didn't hesitate because Lafayette needed me. When I arrived at his unit Lafayette came out right away, and he lit up when he saw me. He thanked me and said, "I love you." I gave him a kiss and a hug and said, "I love *you*." I watched him as he walked back into his unit.

What a gift! To know that in our last moments together, we expressed our love for each other. Smiling at the memory, I looked over at my husband sleeping peacefully and whispered, "Thank you." Through his love, Lionel had helped me welcome God back into my life. Then I looked up to the heavens and said, "Thank you, God!" Through *His* love, I was able to welcome the moments—the heart-wrenching and the joyous, the silly and the somber—back into my life—into my heart.

Kim R. Grimes is an ordained minister, a transformational life coach and a life-changing speaker. Her remarkable messages inspire listeners to shed self-imposed baggage and obstacles that prevent them from living abundantly. She encourages people to identify their phobias, overcome their fears, achieve their goals and live their dreams. Kim retired as a Major from the United States Army Reserves after twenty-five years. She is also the founder of Living Abundantly, Inc., Inspiring the Teen Spirit, Inc. and Life Abundant Enrichment Center, Inc. Connect with Kim at www. KimRGrimes.com.

Tiffanie Y. Lewis

Cold, Hard Steel

A woman touched my arm as I walked from the major department store and out into the mall. "Excuse me, miss." I turned and saw a familiar face. My whole body felt warm. My two friends turned to hear the woman say, "Come with me." I don't recall her saying, "please." I looked at my friends, terrified. I thought I knew what the woman wanted, but they had no idea. The thin, blonde woman, dressed in jeans, t-shirt and beige jacket, had a small purse strapped across her chest. *Where had I seen her before?*

She led me through the store to a back hallway and then to a small office with off-white walls. I can't remember the details of our conversation, but as she was talking I remembered where I had seen her. She had been sitting in the department store dressing room while I was trying on clothes. Now she was here asking me to reveal what I had stolen from the department store. She left me in the room to allow me to undress. I felt like I was going to vomit everything I had eaten for the last three months onto the floor!

I took off my black raincoat and then my black and green sweater, and looked down to my breasts and the two bras I had on—mine and the one I took off the hanger in the dressing room. It was white. I don't know why; I just wanted a white underwear set. *Well,* I thought, *you're not getting one today.* I slipped it off and laid it on a chair. I felt like I was watching someone else's life, like a scene from a movie. An embarrassing scene.

She returned with a white, male police officer in uniform. *Uh oh.* The woman was a plainclothes officer; she asked me if I was sure that the bra was all I had.

Horrified, I lied and told her "yes." I just couldn't bring myself to tell her I had on the matching panties.

The next thing I knew, the male officer was telling me to put my hands behind my back, clasping handcuffs on me, and reciting my rights. "You have the right to remain silent," he said. *The right?* I couldn't fix my lips to express anything. *I can't believe this is happening. How did I get here?* As the male officer led me out of that office and outside, a million thoughts raced. *How did the*

The next thing I knew, the male officer was telling me to put my hands behind my back, clasping handcuffs on me, and reciting my rights.

---

female officer figure me out? Did I look suspicious? Where are my friends? What am I going to tell my parents? Most of all, I felt sad that I couldn't go back in time and tell my friend who introduced me to the five-finger discount that it was a stupid idea and I would have no part in it.

The officer had put my coat around my shoulders and closed the button on the front near my neck so passersby couldn't see the handcuffs, but I could feel them. The cold, hard steel around my wrists sent a message to me that the law is for the lawless, and the lawless person in those metal rings was not the person I was in my heart.

How did I get here? How did I get here? The officer led me to the police car and opened the back door.

He drove to the mall's police station. All I remember is black fingers and a flash of light—fingerprints and photographs. I was told I'd have a hearing, and then I was released, back into the mall.

My friends met me with tons of questions. I know that I answered them, but I was so consumed with my own thoughts that their voices seemed to fade into the background as we drove home.

When I got home I prayed that nobody was there. It seemed quiet enough, but I couldn't tell. I began crying uncontrollably, as if my tear ducts held an unlimited supply of salt water. Did I have to tell my parents?

I continued to weep as I took off my clothes. I looked at those white rayon and polyester panties, with their damask design, as if they had been dipped in sewer water. *So much for having pure,*

Did I have to tell my parents?

---

white underwear, I thought as I threw them in the dresser drawer. Within a few hours I had confessed to my mother through sobs, stuttering, my head hanging low. It's a good thing I decided to come clean, because I was a minor; and within a few days the police had called to inform my parents that I had a hot date with a judge.

My father drove me to the hearing. We had taken many road trips together in the past, and I remembered a conversation we had when I was eight years old. My cousin wanted to fight me in school, and when my father got wind of it, he said to me, "What's your last name?"

I answered, "Lewis."

Then he exclaimed, "You carry *my* name, and you must always remember that our name is a great name." Now, in the car, I could sense my father's disappointment. I hadn't lived up to our name. I had tarnished it.

In the courtroom, I waited with bated breath for my turn to approach the judge. When my name was called, I couldn't feel my legs, but somehow I managed to stand up and walk toward the man in the black robe. My father stood and followed me through the bar—the short wooden swinging doors that separated the law in action from the viewing public.

"Are you her lawyer?" the judge asked my father.

"No," he replied, "I'm her father." I breathed a sigh of relief when I heard my father's voice. I was nervous, but I wasn't alone.

"Well, unless you're her lawyer and going to defend her, you need to step back behind the bar," the judge instructed. I immediately felt tense, almost abandoned, as I glanced behind me. My father was still there, standing just "on the other side of those swinging doors.

The judge explained that my offense was considered a misdemeanor and not a felony. That was a little comforting, because I knew a felony was a more serious crime. Then, the judge took away that little comfort. "Young lady, for this offense you could spend up to ninety days in jail." Ninety days?!

At that moment, you might think that my life flashed before my eyes; but it wasn't my life that flashed before me. Instead, clips from the movie *My Future* played in my mind. If I went to jail for ninety days, I would miss the prom. I would miss graduating tenth in my class. I could lose my full-tuition scholarship. Oh, no! I wouldn't get these stupid braces off! *I cannot go to jail!* I yelled in my mind. *Who is this person standing in front of this judge? This isn't right. I shouldn't be here. I should be preparing for college and my career, not for confinement because of foolish shoplifting. How did I get here?*

I got here because I didn't have the courage to be me. My own thoughts were drowned out by the voices of others telling me that I was just not cool enough. I didn't use drugs. I had more dreams about sex than actual experiences. I had no desire to drink alcohol. I generally got along with everyone. I just didn't have friends that I thought I really fit with. So I did what every teenager tries to do at some point—find a group to fit in with.

As a result, I had adopted the ideas of others as my own—and that had landed me in front of this judge. I suddenly, finally, realized that I wasn't being fully myself, but a version of myself, with certain friends.

I decided at that moment: *I will not stand in this place again. I have to be my own person. I have to listen to my heart. I have to follow my own voice. I have to make a powerful choice! Besides, why would I insult God, who created me, by trying to be like someone else?*

"There's only one reason why I'm not sending you to jail today," the judge said, startling me. "Do you know why?"

"No," I managed to let the word slip from my quivering lips.

"It's because of that man right there," he explained, as he pointed to my father. The judge went on to say that because my father was with me, he knew that I had someone who cared enough about me to lead me in the right direction.

After I left the courtroom, I decided what I did not want for my life, most especially "friends" who thought shoplifting was cool. I wanted to live up to the name my father gave me. To avoid what I didn't want, I needed a plan for what I did want. My plan. No

---

*We all have champions in our lives who
guide us valiantly from victory to victory.*

---

one else's. Dale Carnegie wrote the book, *How to Win Friends and Influence People.* When I left the courtroom, I was on a different mission: "How to Lose Friends and Influence Yourself."

We all have champions in our lives who guide us valiantly from victory to victory. Sometimes a champion's work is to save your life so you can make it to your next victory. My father was my champion that year—he saved my life. He helped me renew my faith in who I was. His presence kept me from going to jail. He then pointed me in the direction of my first job out of high school, which catapulted my career.

Fifteen years later I have traveled internationally, teaching, training and facilitating workshops for a multi-national Fortune 500 Company. I am a published author, a licensed evangelist missionary and an aspiring entrepreneur.

At seventeen years old, I experienced both the worst year of my life and the best year of my life. It was an opportunity to recognize the power of choice. I accepted the fact that I was raised to take a spiritual approach to life, to listen to the *yes* or *no* from my own soul, and to march to the beat of my own drum. We design our path to destiny with every choice we make. At a young age we have the power, the freedom, to choose.

Every *yes* we say within ourselves that leads us to a behavior or action is just as important as every *no*. Most importantly, even if a *yes* leads us to a place we don't want to be, if we are blessed to open our eyes another day, we have the power to make one more choice.

Tiffanie Y. Lewis, founder of Love 1 Ministries, has counseled hundreds of teens and young adults to live their best relationships in a beautiful spiritual triangle with God. With God always on Tiffanie's shoulder, she is a sought-after inspirational keynote speaker, Bible study leader and workshop facilitator. Close to her heart is her mission to help teens, young adults and women unlock their hidden potential through self-love, self-discovery and the practical application of biblical principles. Her degrees are in psychology and business. Connect with Tiffanie at www.Tiffanie-Y-Lewis.com

Veronica Butler, MD

Are You Listening to Your Inner Wisdom?

In 1996, while perusing a favorite catalog, I came across a beautiful bracelet that I knew my mother would love. It was everything she was: refined, beautiful and practical. I was sure it would be incredibly expensive, too expensive for my budget, but it was on sale at an amazingly low price.

Feeling almost dizzy at my good fortune, I pulled out my credit card and bought the bracelet right then and there over the phone. Valentine's Day was right around the corner, and I was sure this bracelet would make the perfect gift.

But then I thought, "Sale or no sale, this is way too much money to spend on a Valentine's Day gift." It seemed a better idea to save the pricey bracelet for my mother's birthday, which was in May. My new and improved plan was so logical: I would wait and give her the bracelet in May.

Later that day, as I was getting out of my car at the office, I started hearing a James Taylor song in my head. The song was "Shower the People You Love with Love," a tune I knew well and loved: "Just shower the people you love with love/ show them the way you feel...."

At first I thought it was charming to be reminded of such a great song. I thought about how cute James Taylor had been in his prime, how much I liked the tune, and how beautiful the message was. At one point I even caught myself swaying to the music, letting myself get carried away with the rhythm and melody playing in my head as I went about my daily activities.

After a week though, when the song didn't stop but actually became LOUDER and more frequent, I grew a little distressed by its persistence. What was going on? There was no reasonable explanation for the song's repetition—and yet, try as I might to ignore it, it was still there.

A few days later I decided to send the bracelet on Valentine's Day rather than wait until my mother's birthday in May. It was a subtle and quick decision. There were no fireworks involved, no

I remember how warm, loving and loved I felt during that phone call.

major drama, no soul searching, I just woke up one day and said to myself, "Just send the bracelet now."

As soon as I made the decision, the music stopped playing in my head. Abruptly. A sweet wave of relief washed over me, but I wouldn't understand the connection between this wonderful feeling and the decision to send the bracelet on Valentine's Day until later.

I remember being so excited when I wrapped and sent the bracelet to my mother in Michigan. I just knew she was going to love it, and the thought of her opening the package and embracing this symbol of my love for her made me very happy. I waited in giddy anticipation, and then finally called her on Valentine's Day.

Although we lived in different states, my mother and I visited each other often throughout the year, and we usually spoke on the phone a couple of times a week. Our conversations were always light and loving, but this call was especially sweet. I wished her a happy Valentine's Day and asked if she liked the gift. She gushed over how beautiful it was, and how she would cherish it forever. Grinning from ear to ear, I was bursting with joy and pride that I had pleased her so much.

I remember how warm, loving and loved I felt during that phone call. The flow of our exchange was so sweet and pure, there were moments when I couldn't tell who was speaking and who was listening. The pauses and silences in our conversation were filled with joy, love and gratitude. As the conversation ended, we giggled for several minutes and told each other how much we loved each other. Then we hung up.

She died two days later.

The grief was palpable, my heart literally ached; I was disoriented, not knowing what to do. I tried to anchor myself in my responsibilities. My mother had been a bright light in my life, the ultimate role model, eternally wise, faithful and strong. She had given me a powerful sense of "how things should be" and a set of high moral guidelines she considered inviolable rules of life. But

---

She taught me that the source of wisdom, love and strength was all within, and reminded me that we can all have contact with that source.

---

most importantly, she had taught me to *trust the guidance of my own inner voice.* Remembering that, suddenly everything fell into place. I remembered the James Taylor tune, the timing of sending the bracelet, the song vanishing, our joyful last conversation and the perfect love that we had shared in that final phone call.

Before my mother died, I once commented on how lucky she was to have a doting, loving husband to care for her in her illness. She really surprised me when she responded that, yes, she appreciated the supportive attention from my father and loved him dearly, but when it came down to it, "It's just between you and God." She taught me that the source of wisdom, love and strength was all within, and reminded me that we can all have contact with that source.

During one of our phone conversations several years before her death, she—out of the blue—told me that Jesus had visited her and told her that I should write a book. I was super busy, a divorced mom, had a solo practice and was teaching at a local university. A bit annoyed, I said, "Yeah, yeah, okay, Mother—" mostly to placate her.

A couple of days later, I received a call from two friends of mine telling me they needed help writing a book they were working on about Ayurvedic medicine (the natural medicine of India) and had thought of me. My mother's words came rushing back and I agreed to help. The book, *A Woman's Best Medicine,* is now a published work. I would never have agreed to co-author it if it hadn't been for

*I realized that the inner voice was simply
the voice of Nature speaking to me,
showing me the divine order of things.*

my mother's message. And now that I think about it, who was I to argue with Jesus, hectic schedule or not? I was beginning to learn how to honor the intuitive life my mother had lived, and I realized that the inner voice was simply the voice of Nature speaking to me, showing me the divine order of things.

Intuition, that inner wisdom, often flies in the face of logic and reason. It can at times seem crazy in the short term, but it has never failed me in the long term. Ever. As a matter of fact, it has on many occasions protected me from irreparable harm and catastrophic error—the bracelet incident being one such occasion.

It happened on another occasion when I was in college, and failing French. A friend who was majoring in French offered to take my final for me. I never for a moment considered accepting; it flew in the face of all the natural laws my mother had taught me and I refused. I failed the final. Later, when speaking to my counselor about my potential career paths, she noticed that my math and science grades were so high that I could easily get into medical school. Becoming a medical doctor had never even registered on my radar as a goal for my future, but suddenly, there it was. I grabbed the opportunity with both hands and eventually obtained my degree.

I can't imagine how awful I would have felt if I had "saved" the gift for May and not been able, in a very special way, to show my mother how much I loved her and how grateful I was to her for being such a wonderful person and great mother. This was the lesson of the song. Once I surrendered to its message, I was able to open my heart to love and gratitude and ignore the limits of logic. This was the inner wisdom at work. Inner wisdom is always at work, we just have to learn to be receptive to it.

My sister and daughter say they get visits from my mother in their times of need, but for me, my mother's visits have quieted. That doesn't sadden me. I miss her, and yes, sometimes I still cry when I think of her, but the loss is manageable now. Her voice is quiet, but mine is strong and clear. It sounds silly sometimes to speak about my inner voice publicly. As a matter of fact, my mother warned me against doing just that. "People will think you're crazy, Veronica!" she used to say.

I think my mother's presence has receded because I was able to finally learn all the lessons she wanted to teach me; how to surrender to the wisdom of life, how to follow the natural laws, how to trust my inner voice, and how to always, always, listen for the universal music that guides, loves and protects. No matter how crazy it may sound.

I have the bracelet now. I keep it close. It reminds me of my mother; a beautiful gem with many facets of wisdom and knowledge. Its exquisite craftsmanship reminds me of my mother's refined grace and unique quality of character. Its solid exterior reminds me of my mother's moral strength, and the way the light shines through its stones reminds me of my mother's inner light, a light that shone on me and everyone lucky enough to know her. She gently drew out my light so that I might share it with the world. I am constantly reminded that I must do the same for my own daughter and myself. You must do it for yourself.

Veronica Butler, MD is the proud mother of the fashion designer Wells Butler Nathan. Veronica is Medical Director and owner of the Family Medical Center in Ottumwa, Iowa; Adjunct Professor, Clinical Faculty at the University of Des Moines; and Medical Director of the Women's Health Institute—The Raj Fairfield in Iowa. She earned her BS from the University of Michigan and her medical degree from Howard University, and did postgraduate work in public health at the University of Michigan. Since 1975, she has been practicing Transcendental Meditation. Veronica co-authored the book A Woman's Best Medicine (Tarcher/Putnam Publishing). Connect with Veronica at www.StayInTheNow.com

Christie Sheldon

Earning My "A"

*Y**ou hear stories about this happening to people,* I thought. *It always sounded totally exaggerated. But now it's* actually *happening to* me!

I wasn't sure how I had even come to be standing in front of my college speech class of about forty-five fellow students, with our teacher, Mrs. Olsen, sitting right in the middle of the group. I stared out into that separate world, and I could see forty-six bored, teenage faces, forty-six pairs of eyes staring right back at me through the dim fluorescent light.

I had been a little nervous in the morning, but that was totally normal; I was about to give my first speech ever, after all, and it had to be a whole thirty minutes long. I had worked hard on it, even memorized it, going over my index cards and reading them in my lap in the car on the way to class, and I felt pretty confident throughout the day.

When I got up in front of the class, however, it all changed, and I started to panic.

Just like it happens in the movies, the images in front of my eyes seemed to blur and move into a distorted, tunnel-like shape, as if I were looking at everyone sitting before me through a fishbowl. I felt myself turning as red as a lobster, and I started to shake as my adrenaline kicked in.

My fellow classmates were staring at me, bored out of their gourds and thinking about what they had to say. I blurted out the first three lines of my speech. And then it happened—my worst nightmare. My mind was blank. Literally, NOTHING occurred between my brain and my mouth. I stammered. I froze. I forgot everything, literally *everything* I had prepared for after the first three lines.

I stood stock still for what seemed like forever as everyone started to shuffle around uncomfortably in their seats, staring at the loser in front of them. *I'll do anything to get out of this moment,*

Quitting was not an option. Luckily,
it wasn't hardwired into me.

I thought. *If a lightning bolt could come through the ceiling, that would be amazing. Just get me out of here!*

I scoped out the exit doors on either side of me from where I stood in the front of the class. My eyes shot toward each of them. The one on the right was a little bit closer. *I could just walk right out of here and never come back... get an "F" and just be done with it forever.*

The only problem with this was I couldn't just let myself fail. I was always the responsible one, the one who had been promoted to manager at the restaurant where I worked when I was just sixteen, the one who got good grades in school even while I played sports full time and worked long hours. An "F" was just not going to cut it, because that would mean I had given up. My reputation was on the line. Quitting was not an option. Luckily, it wasn't hardwired into me.

So, I stood there, struck dumb in my fishbowl, looking out and thinking, *If I stand here long enough, maybe the floor will swallow me whole.* Again, my prayers went unanswered. After what felt like five minutes, to my horror, I started mumbling, "I can't remember what to say, I can't remember what to say," over and over again. The teacher said nothing; no one said a word, but everyone continued to stare at the loser in front of them. I could see their thoughts blinking on their foreheads: "Whoa. This girl is totally losing it."

Then I felt a little switch flip inside of me. *What the hell,* I thought. *Just say* something. *If you can't remember this dumb speech, just tell them* something. So I started telling the class about what I thought life should really look like. It had nothing to do with my topic. I didn't apologize; I didn't care anymore. *I already got an "F" in this speech class, I might as well use my moment to tell people what I really think.* So I took the reins, knees wobbling, and started telling my audience what I thought about life, and how it could be better.

"If I could live my life full out and get over all of my fears," I said slowly, looking out at the slack faces, "I'd be really, really happy." I sped up. "Life should not be full of so many obstacles.

So I took the reins, knees wobbling, and started telling my audience what I thought about life, and how it could be better.

Love can change a lot of people's perspectives. Parents should treat their kids like individuals, not compilations of how they view the world. If everyone would just be a cheerleader for each other, things would change on the planet."

Now I was rambling, shaking with fear and adrenaline. Once I got started talking about how I would change the world and what I truly felt inspired by, I could open my heart and start breathing again. I thought it was five minutes, but I spoke for thirty. I have not a clue how the words came out or what most of them were. I just knew I cared about how the world should look.

I would love to say I got a standing ovation—that never happened. No one even clapped for me. Mrs. Olsen glanced at me kindly and said only, "Good."

I bowed my head, mortified, walked to my desk and wished desperately for the bell to ring. *Oh my God, I just got an "F." I got an "F!" What am I going to do?*

A week later, I got my grade. Mrs. Olsen literally gave me an "A" for effort. I was shocked a bit, but as I thought about it, I appreciated her more and more for encouraging me instead of squashing my effort. If I had quit, I would have had an "F." But she gave me an "A" because of where I started (petrified) and for how I finished (I persisted, and I didn't run out of the room). I felt a little guilty for the "A," but I knew I had already lived my worst fear and learned how to move through it: by being true to myself and talking about what I really loved. It could never ever get worse than those first five minutes in front of the class.

A couple years later, at the same Illinois college, I was named Female Athlete of the Year. I had to give a small acceptance speech when I accepted my award. I walked up onstage to cheers and the stomping of many feet and felt so full, so happy: *I did it. I really did it!* I felt so grateful, so proud, I thought I must be glowing visibly.

I transformed my own fear into love. Love is a verb. Love is an active force of nature.

Working, going to school and being an athlete, all full-time, was no small achievement for me. Before I opened my mouth to accept my award, I smiled. *This will be no problem: I'm speaking from the heart.*

"Thank you so much for this award," I said to the cheering audience. "I'm honored, and I'm honored to play on some amazing teams. I accept this award for all of my teammates. I love you guys!"

Since that time, I've realized I'm not that bad as a speaker. For me, communication has to have love and inspiration in it. It has to reach in and grab people and make them think. It's about leading people to conscious, inspired lives… of fun, love and peace vs. quiet desperation.

My life now is about transforming people through workshops that move them into lives they love. This requires me to speak frequently, and sometimes I still get nervous and question my ability to speak with grace and ease. When that happens, I remember the moment that I completely forgot everything. I am reminded that the universe has set me up to always be supported in my next steps, guiding me effortlessly if I just follow through and go for it. I can truly maintain my power, knowing I am always supported.

Every morning feels like Christmas morning to me, as I open my inbox and see the hundreds of inspiring emails from clients who have managed to transform life's limited options into unlimited, loving gifts by using the tools I showed them. Knowing I've helped thousands of these amazing people activates my heart like nothing else. So when I do that through speaking, teaching and healing, that's a blessing to me. That's a well-lived life in my book. What people respect about me is I'll do anything to get that result, move beyond any of my own fears. Today, I've spoken to literally millions of people over the radio, TV and Internet. I transformed my own fear into love. Love is a verb. Love is an active force of nature.

I know I flubbed my first college speech, but I truly believe that Mrs. Olsen saw *something* in me, and like an inspiring cheerleader, she didn't want to squash me any more than I was already squashing myself: Instead, her courtesy "A" inspired me to pick myself up from my immobilizing moment, dust myself off and speak about things that I love.

I get it now, Mrs. Olsen: It's not about just the perfect delivery, pitch, tone and body posture; it's more about the inspired messages that pour from our hearts when we love people enough to care about their lives. It's about sharing tools that help each other live a life we love. It's this inspiration that leaps from my soul that makes speaking up worth it. I thank you, Mrs. Olsen, that today I have truly earned my "A." Many blessings to you for making it easy and safe for me to re-claim.

Christie Sheldon is an intuitive life coach and facilitator for life, love and celebration. For the last decade Christie has helped more than fourteen thousand people to align with their ideal version of life, guiding them to choose the ideal in love, relationships, family, self-esteem, work, money and careers. Christie's program, Living Love or Above, the Toolkit, is a compilation of her teachings, and it comprises a practical set of tools that anyone can use to start raising their energetic vibrancy above the level of love—the level where real shifts occur and one becomes an "instant magnet" for love and abundance.

An acclaimed speaker, Christie is a regular featured guest on top radio and television programs. Her weekly podcasts reach tens of thousands, and her participants in her live webinars exceed fifty thousand. She has been featured with such luminaries as Lisa Nichols, Marci Shimoff, Mariel Hemingway, Jack Canfield, John Gray, Geneen Roth and others. Connect with Christie at www.ChristieSheldon.com.

Felicia Shaw

One Little Bite at a Time

I picked up the envelope from the admissions department from the dinette table in my tiny apartment where I'd been staring at it, sick to my stomach, for hours. *This is going to break me,* I thought, *and everything is going to be over... or maybe there's still a chance.*

With trembling hands, I opened it and saw what I'd known I would see:

This letter is to inform you that you have been placed under academic suspension for the remainder of the school year. Due to poor performance, and following the guidelines of your scholarship to Western Michigan University, your grant monies have been withdrawn. You may again register for classes, without financial aid from this institution, beginning in the next calendar year.

I crumpled into a chair and started to cry. I saw the image of my mother's disappointed face, the faces of the neighborhood friends I'd bragged to: "I'm going to college. I'm going to make a difference."

I grew up in the inner city of Detroit, a skinny kid who was mocked for having big ideas. My single mom sacrificed everything to raise her family with grace and lots of encouragement. It had been a total triumph to be the first person in my family admitted to college.

When I was a little girl, I looked at the people around me who seemed to have the good things in life—a house, a car, a nice-looking family—and they were all accountants. So ever since I was in fifth grade, I knew I wanted to be one, too. When I got into college, I briefly thought about entering the theater department.

It had been a total triumph to be the first person in my family admitted to college.

But then I looked at the statistics and thought, *This opportunity is too precious—I can't waste it. Theater is a difficult field to get a job in, and most people have to work for minimum wage while waiting for that big opportunity given only to the best.* I wasn't confident that I was the best, so I went ahead and declared a major in accounting.

I always did okay in math, and the first couple years in college went pretty well. During those years of earning my general credits, I kept a B average. But then I finally got into my core accounting classes. After my first semester in it I realized, *I hate accounting! Am I* really *going to do this for the rest of my life?*

I'm an extrovert. I love to talk to and associate with people, and I actually wound up joining a couple of organizations centered around accounting in school to feed that extrovert in me—but the more I got involved in that world, the less I liked it. It was sickening to realize I was looking down a dark tunnel, not a path of fulfillment. And I got terrible headaches just thinking: *You're going to be in this career for at least twenty years. And every day, more than likely, you're going to work by yourself, which you don't like; you love being with people. And you're going to crunch numbers when you don't even really care for numbers.*

Feeling totally trapped, I became very depressed. *Oh my God, I've already used up two years in college, and this is my major. I hate this—I don't want this to be my life. But I can't go back.* I really didn't think I *could* go back. So I began to panic every time I tried to study. My heart raced and I began to sweat as I thought, *This is your life. This is your life.* To add to my panic and despair, I didn't understand much of what I was studying. I felt humiliated and worthless. *I must be the dumbest person in the world.*

The slightest thing drew my attention away from my studies, and my grades started to slip. I felt my anxiety building, but I still couldn't focus. To build up my low self-confidence, I spent as much time with my friends and in school groups as I could. I felt better about myself when I was distracted from thinking about my major, my inability to understand the materials, my future and my rapidly slipping grade point average. It was down to a "D" by the time the letter arrived from the admissions department.

After I got the letter, I cried for days, so hard I thought I would throw up. I kept going to work but didn't tell anyone what had happened. I kept my head down, afraid to make eye contact in case I burst into tears. I was so social, everyone must have thought I was

---

After I got the letter, I cried for days, so hard I thought I would throw up.

---

acting very strange. *I'm that person they talked about in middle school. I'm just dumb, I'm never going to be anything. I've let my mother down because of my selfishness. I've let so many people down, including myself. How can I face them? How can I go forward?*

Finally, I had to tell my mom I was no longer in school. I couldn't bring myself to tell her the truth; I just told her my grant money was no longer available. She cared so much about me, had worked so hard to encourage me. "I'm sure you've done your best, Felicia," she said in her gentle voice, and I felt like I might die of regret and shame: *I did this to myself!* "You can always come back home. You can work and save up money until you can afford to go back to school."

But I couldn't go back to Detroit. Without an education, there wasn't a chance of success. Many people I knew back there partied hardcore so they could forget the sadness and inequities of life. I knew that if I went back there, I would not go back to school. And I would live in a state of constant regret.

I didn't know what I was going back to school for, but I knew I had to do it. There was no other choice. I had always been told, and had always thought, that without an education the most I could probably do was work a fast food job and live paycheck-to-weekend. But if I wanted something different, if I wanted better for myself, I had to have a college education. *By any means necessary, I have to graduate, with a degree. I need to have a career. I don't want just a job—I want a career. Failure is NOT an option.*

So I had to take a hard look at my life and make a plan. How was I going to make ends meet with no grant? *First things first: I need to work full-time.* I had two jobs, but they paid minimum

---

I burst into tears. For the first time in my life, I cried because I was happy.

---

wage, and the bills kept coming. How much was it going to take to get out of debt? I wrote my creditors and made arrangements. I even got on welfare. I had to lose my embarrassment and just admit that I needed the help.

It was at Social Services that someone first said, "There's more for you to do than just accounting." That rang a bell. *You know what? You're right!* I started looking into other options and got a third job working in a factory at night to save up money for school because I still didn't have enough for tuition. I had no choice. My mother had always told me I would need to sacrifice and work hard for what I wanted.

Then I heard that the university was hiring a secretary. I got the job! My windows opened again: working there meant I got a seventy-five percent discount on tuition. I started slowly, with one class, one bite, at a time. I thought, *This is good! And it's okay if it takes six years to graduate.* I just kept working and thinking, *I want better for me. There IS better for me.* As I saw results, I felt my self-confidence growing and taking shape.

The other great thing about the job was that I was working in a department where someone took the time to talk to me about all the different majors, all the different choices that would match my personality. I enthusiastically latched onto human resources, because it would always give me a chance to talk with others, to help them develop, to provide them with the kind of help I had once needed so badly.

When I got the letter that contained my first grade from my first class in my new life in school, I was so nervous I felt like I might pass out. I opened it, looked at the grade, shook my head to clear my vision and looked again. I couldn't believe it. I ran over to admissions and asked them to verify it. "Yes, that's an 'A,'" the woman at the desk said, smiling. I burst into tears. For the first time in my life, I cried because I was happy.

I remembered what my mother had taught me: "You just need to believe it can be, and do the work—just believe in yourself, Felicia, and make the effort."

It had worked! I truly believed: *I CAN be the person I want to be! I AM smart enough.* When I called my mom to say, "I'm graduating on THIS day," I felt so much pride and joy I was smiling from ear to ear. Something deep inside me had changed.

Today, in my forties with an MBA under my belt, I love myself and feel comfortable in my own skin. I'm not afraid of failure anymore. Now, when something looks challenging, I know I have to keep focused and take tiny bites rather than try to digest it all at once. I know I will get past it—I just close my eyes and remember what it felt like to achieve what I wanted for the first time, that "A," and tell myself, *If I can conquer this, just one little bite at a time, I'll have that same, wonderful feeling.*

Felicia Shaw enjoys working to improve communities as a high achiever's life coach and motivational speaker who empowers professionals' overall development through her business, Simply In Your Purpose. She has also done this through her work at State Farm for over seventeen years (the past ten as a public affairs specialist). Felicia received her BBA in human resource management and MBA in strategic management from Western Michigan University; her coaching certification from the ICF-accredited Coach Training Alliance; and her ATM and CL designations through Toastmasters International.

Felicia hosts Minding My Business, *a radio show for entrepreneurs that airs every Wednesday at 6 PM on WXRJ 94.9 in Bloomington/Normal. Among other volunteer activities, she serves as Vice Chair of the McLean County Urban League's board and coordinates programs in her local graduate chapter of Sigma Gamma Rho Sorority, Inc. Connect with Felicia at www.SimplyInYourPurpose.com.*

Patti Waterbury

Coming Out of the Dark

My heart sank as my doctor scribbled his signature on the medical leave request form. *How can this be happening again? I just led a six-billion-dollar acquisition integration and now I can barely get dressed and make it to a doctor's appointment?*

Although the business transition had been successful, twelve months of eighteen-hour days had taken their toll. Beyond burnout, I felt like a "crispy critter." I was unable to eat or sleep, and the loss of twenty-five pounds was a clear sign that the cloud of depression had overtaken me.

"Thank you," I whispered, as I folded the paper and stuck it in my purse. I took a deep breath. *It's okay, Patti, you just need rest.*

On my way to the car, my phone rang. My sister's voice was tense and urgent. "Patti, the doctor wants Mom admitted to the hospital tonight... he says we can't afford to wait." My heart sank. *No! This can't be happening!*

Over the next sixteen months, I watched my hero and biggest cheerleader lose the battle for her life. The anticipation of the loss intensified my fear and anger. *If this is how God treats someone who serves Him faithfully for fifty years, I don't have a snowball's chance in hell.* Each day that I spent with her—listening as she shared her faith, wisdom and stories, seeing the lives she still touched—I was struck again by the emptiness of my own existence. She was losing her life to cancer, and yet she was more vibrant and alive than I was.

Yes, I had traveled the world, training leaders and solving problems for a Fortune 500 company. But while I appeared successful, my youthful dreams of marriage, raising a family and changing lives as my parents had done had become the price of my success. And now, my new boss in the company I had given my life to showed no compassion and was quickly losing confidence in me.

My mom's condition was terminal; my own body refused to heal. The son I had committed to raise needed a mom, but my

---

She was losing her life to cancer, and yet
she was more vibrant and alive than I was.

---

ability to care for him was debatable. For the third time in my life, the thick black cloud began to suffocate the life out of me.

I was fifteen the first time the cloud descended. As a teenager, I usually thought more and felt more deeply than I was willing to share. My natural affect was flat, so people often encouraged me to smile. I usually acted like I ignored them, but inside I was screaming, *I'll smile when I damn well feel like it!* I tried to prove my value through sports, but when I didn't perform well, the voice in my head was ruthless. I let music give voice to the pain I felt inside as I listened to "Ooh, dream weaver/ I believe you can get me through the night," and "Don't want to be/ all by myself anymore" over and over again.

The dark cloud appeared again when I was twenty-eight and a successful professional. As a support group leader for people struggling with chemical abuse and codependency, I was asked to attend an intensive workshop designed to resolve life issues. Committed to leading by example, I naïvely agreed. I had no idea it would force the emotions I had long neglected to emerge. Cries of anguish broke my silence and a flash flood of tears engulfed my soul, running down my face in easy streams. The illusion of my "have it all together" life shattered at my feet. I realized that I didn't have the skills or emotional stamina I needed to cope with how I honestly felt about my life, and I checked myself in to the hospital.

During the pre-admission interview the nurse asked me, "Do you have a suicide plan?"

I replied, "Which one do you want?" It wasn't that I wanted to die; I just didn't want to live this way anymore. I had multiple suicide plans: I could drive my car into a wall; take a bullet to the head; overdose. What stopped me? I feared that suicide would be akin to jumping out of the frying pan and into the fire. Though my relationship to God was fragile, the possibility of eternal separation was still a powerful deterrent. Even so, I was on suicide watch the first few days in treatment, and so shut down that it took me ten weeks to complete a six-week program. During that time, I became

---

*It wasn't that I wanted to die; I just
didn't want to live this way anymore.*

---

more able to recognize my feelings and separate my own worth from the failure or success of my actions. I discovered that, aside from the chemical imbalance in my brain, my depression had been further complicated by my pattern of turning my anger inward. I finally grasped that feelings aren't bad; it's what you do with them that counts.

After several months, I went back to work filled with a renewed sense of purpose. But periodically the cloud of depression emerged. Amidst the stress of worrying about losing my job and the deep grief surrounding my mom's illness, I lost sight of the sun. Something snapped inside and I slipped back into living as a fractured person—one kind of person at work, another at home.

The anger and fear continued to express itself painfully in my body. The frequency of panic attacks increased as my mom's health declined. I tried to be a mother to a five year-old boy who had already lost two mothers, while desperately trying to cut through the mental fog every day to be productive at work and keep my job.

My new routines as a caregiver and a mom, combined with work, felt impossible.

My body eventually said, *"You quit, or I'll quit!"* When I finally resigned myself to the impending loss of my job, I did the unthinkable; I underwent three major surgical procedures at once to try to ensure that my health wouldn't be a deterrent in a future role. I felt I had no choice; even though I knew that my mom probably wouldn't be with us for more than a few weeks, I had to do it before I lost my insurance coverage.

I was right. Two weeks after surgery, emotionally bankrupt and barely able to stand the physical pain long enough to make it through airport security, I made my final trip to see her. One

---

With gratitude, I take a deep breath and
embrace the preciousness of each new day.

---

short week later, she was gone. Without her presence as the glue in our family, we dealt with our pain separately. Combined with everything else, that loss left me in an emotional free-fall.

I was nowhere near able to return to work when short-term disability ran out; long-term disability was my only remaining option. My psychiatrist said, "Patti, I've never seen anyone come back from long-term disability in a situation like this." Though his words slapped me in the face, the compassion in his eyes spoke volumes.

"Then I'll be your first one." The strength of my tone surprised both of us. His words awoke something deep inside of me. I refused to give in to the darkness that had already stolen years of my life. The stakes were different this time. I had promised Trystan that I would be his last mother. So I knew I had to get down to the core of this problem once and for all, for him as much as for me.

"God, I am mad as hell that you let Mom die. I don't love You; in fact, I don't even like You right now. But it's clear that I'm not going to make it without You, so please heal my mind and help me get my life back together. I am looking up, but I can't even see bottom from here and don't trust myself anymore. Please, God," I pleaded, "Please help me pick up all the pieces of my life and give me the desire and courage to put them back together again."

Over the next four months, thanks to an "earth angel" who directed an outpatient program, I had a safe place to begin to heal. As the cloud slowly dissipated and my life got back on track, I aligned my personal and professional dreams so that I would never again sacrifice one at the cost of the other. Spiritual healing has been an integral part of my healing process. In the light of His Presence, I can look beyond the shadows of depression and see the strength and compassion I have developed through brokenness. And now my life's work is helping individuals and organizations be their best and do what they are called to do.

Now, in addition to work, my eighteen-hour days include cooking out with Trystan, cheering for my nephews' teams and a little down time for me. I still find great comfort in music, but now "coming out of the dark" plays full volume in my head as the Master Creator's love warms my soul. With gratitude, I take a deep breath and embrace the preciousness of each new day.

Patti Waterbury, founder of Creative Growth Strategies, is a transformational speaker, bestselling author and discerning business coach. A master at orchestrating change, Patti passionately cultivates a kingdom mindset in leaders through biblical principles, proven business approaches and behavioral practices that transform lives, improve organizations and, ultimately, influence nations. Building on a master's in organization development and change management, her commitment to be the student first allows her to stay cutting-edge. With more than twenty years as an organizational troubleshooter and executive coach to Fortune 500 business leaders, entrepreneurs and directors of nonprofits, Patti's diverse academic background and experience give her a unique ability to discern core problems, clarify choices and influence decisions to deliver desired results. Connect with Patti at www.PattiWaterbury.com.

Nina CJ Boykin Jr.

Don't Let Anybody Tell You Your Dreams Are Too Big

I grew up one of eleven children in a small apartment in the projects at Lexington and 110th, an area of Manhattan vividly described in the documentary *American Gangster*.

It was called "El Barrio" then. As a child it seemed to me that my community, which stretched from 110th to 116th Streets along Lexington, was a sea of people without ambitions, people whose hands were swollen from heroin injections and who could barely stand up straight. Still, every morning I heard a voice: "What do you want to be when you grow up?"

I knew the answer. Moreover, I knew another life was possible. I knew this because I had a secret source of information on alternative lifestyles. Well, it was no secret, really; it was broadcast weekly on national television. *The Cosby Show* showed me well-adjusted, successful, upper-middle class black people in a loving, nuclear family and an abiding marriage between two professionals, a doctor and a lawyer.

Throughout my childhood, this program made me believe that I too could have that kind of lifestyle; that my children would not have to live as I lived. Incredibly, the Cosby's helped give me the absolute determination I needed to persevere and overcome the obstacles that lay ahead. And I watched every single episode of the spin-off program, *A Different World,* because it showed black students pursuing their dreams of education.

The professionals who showed up at my school for the seventh grade career fair asked us all the same question: "What do you want to be when you grow up?"

They were much amused when I promptly responded, "I want to be an accountant and manager in a Fortune 500 company."

"Very good, great," they all said. "But you might be setting your goals too high. Why don't you consider being a receptionist at Gimbel's Department Store?" Better that this little black/Latina girl from El Barrio should have realistic expectations. On the way home that afternoon I got beat up, and my assailants stole my coat. I returned to the small unit in the projects where we all lived—

I knew another life was possible.

---

eleven brothers and sisters, with one bathroom—bruised, angry, cold and having been told that my dream was not possible. I could feel the hurt, fear and frustration running through my veins like my blood. *I dare them to try and steal my dreams like those thugs stole my coat! My coat might be available for the taking, but my dreams will NOT be stolen.*

Every morning from that day forth, I got up early and renewed my promise to myself: *Nina, you can be whatever you want to be. Today you are one step closer to living your dreams.*

My school wasn't challenging me, so I got into a better one, far from where I lived. I received assistance for the train fare, but my parents didn't have the extra nickel I needed to take the bus from the train station, so every morning of high school, I got up at five a.m. so I would have time to walk several miles from the train to the school.

I did well, and was awarded a scholarship to Penn State. But my journey began to take some unexpected twists and turns. I still remember my astonishment at the train station when I saw my first Quakers. The person on the Quaker Oats package was real! Pennsylvania was a world so strange to me that I soon found myself back in New York, where I finished college. By nineteen I was married, and soon after, pregnant, broke and barely getting by. I never stopped reminding myself of my original promise.

I had to tap into my bounce-back muscles like never before when my son decided to come into this world prematurely. During thirty-six hours of unbelievably difficult childbirth, I kept worrying, *How in the hell am I going to raise a black man in today's society? How am I going to raise a son who does not become a statistic—dead or incarcerated by his early twenties? How can I even feed him?*

The delivery got even more difficult. The doctor asked my husband to leave the room, then turned to me and asked the most frightening question I had ever been asked. "Nina, whose life do I save, yours or your son's?"

For a second I could not even comprehend the question. Then I heard myself speak with certainty and resolve: "Save my child."

I made the next eighteen years of my life about fostering his success.

Though I was ready to give up my life for my child, I wasn't ready to die yet. I had a promise to keep to myself, and my beautiful little boy to raise. I wanted to teach him: *Dare to dream so BIG that you surprise yourself.* Both my son and I went home; and with my husband Norman by my side, I made the next eighteen years of my life about fostering his success.

I had a job at Gimbel's, as our Career Day guests had recommended and within two weeks said "what the hell?" For that reason and others, I worked harder. I kept chanting my promise to myself that I could be anything that I wanted to be—all the way to a Vice President position at Morgan Stanley. My husband and I bought a house in the suburbs of New Jersey. Since the public school system seemed to be committed to classifying Tyvonne as ADHD, ADD or just BAD and "un-teachable," I made sure he heard me say often, "Son, you can be anything you want to be regardless of what people think. Surprise them." Even though I worked long hours, I was there to push him when his grades dropped.

I worked eighty-hour weeks to climb the corporate ladder, plus teacher conferences, late-night homework and constant encouragement for my son when he felt discouraged. Each day I reminded myself: *Today I am one step closer to living my dreams.* Each new school year, I showed up and introduced myself to each successive teacher: "Hello, I'm Nina CJ Boykin Jr. I have a lot of energy; my goal is to raise a successful man and I am going to be very involved in my son's education." Year after year, I showed up to say, "This young man WILL have an amazing future, and I am here to make sure everyone around him supports him." I fought to keep Tyvonne from being labeled, and I fought to keep them from giving him medication.

One day Tyvonne told me he wanted to be a Boy Scout. I made him keep a book of his goals and dreams. I told him, "Write it down in your book." Even though I knew that being a Boy Scout was not a traditional experience for African, American boys, I wanted Tyvonne to be anything BUT traditional. Off he went, serving as the only black kid in his troop for several years. He was committed, and soon was honored and achieved the rank of Eagle Scout in West Orange, New Jersey. The first in our family. One dream checked off the list—many more to go!

Later, Tyvonne came to me and said, "Mom, I am going to be a research biochemist." *What? Is he insane? Surely he wants to work in the world of finance, where there's money to be made.* For a moment, I forgot my promise to myself and to Tyvonne, and I attempted to steer his dream down a path that I felt was more desirable for him.

"I have friends," I told him. "I can help you."

"Mom, I am going to be a *chemist*."

Suddenly, I realized that, like the ignorant counselors who tried to decide my future in the seventh grade, I was telling my son what his dream should be. I made peace with his decision. After touring a number of campuses, he came back home with news. He wanted to be a Morehouse man. I smiled, remembering that the college in *A Different World* was based on an HBCU similar to Morehouse. I envisioned the Cosby's proudly sending their family to college. I knew that even though we would have to work really, really hard to get him accepted to and finance an education at Morehouse, I was even more confident that I was up for the journey as it was now OUR dream. I said, "Son, if that is your dream, you are going to Morehouse."

His counselors told him he didn't have the grades, and that he should apply to some state universities. I kept reminding him: "You can be anything that you decide to be." But when April of Tyvonne's senior year rolled around and he still hadn't been admitted

---

*I found myself overwhelmed
with pride and triumph.*

---

anywhere, I started to think perhaps his counselors had been right. A local county college or university would be much more practical and affordable. On April 19, Tyvonne rushed into my office and handed me a fat envelope from Morehouse. I read slowly, holding my breath, "We are pleased to accept you into Morehouse College. " *We did it! He won't be a statistic, on medication or a high school dropout. He is going to be a Morehouse man, a college graduate!*

We went to the Morehouse freshman orientation and welcoming ceremonies for the class of 2014 and their parents. To my surprise the keynote speaker was… Mr. Bill Cosby. As much as I tried to remain composed, when I saw him; when I remembered my seventh grade experience, my unwillingness to compromise, my difficult birth and the choice to save my son's life, our fight to keep him off brain-killing medication, and his hard work to bring up his grades so that we all could experience this moment, I found myself overwhelmed with pride and triumph.

Growing up in El Barrio, I learned to survive by being tough and not showing emotion; my children had never seen me cry—he was startled by my unfamiliar behavior. I was crying in the middle of the campus. My son, much taller than me now, came over and cradled my head in his arms. "Mom," he said, "You can't do this.

We're from New York." In that moment, I didn't need to be the strongest person around, or the most successful. I simply basked in my son's promise to *himself* that he could do anything that he wanted to—and did!

A few months later, after a long day at work, I was wondering if I had made the right decision, borrowing against my home and retirement fund to pay Tyvonne's tuition, when I literally bumped into Felicia Rashad, my childhood heroine and star of *The Cosby Show*. In our brief conversation, she mentioned that she had a son who attended Morehouse. I said to her proudly, "So do I." And to myself I said, "Oh yes, we had a dream."

Nina CJ Boykin Jr. is the President and CEO of The Boykin Dream Project, a movement encouraging people to Dare2Dream out loud. She is also a Vice President at Morgan Stanley. Nina is a member of the National Association of Black Accountants, Inc., and leverages her knowledge of business and finance to offer strategies and empower people to rise up and make their dreams a reality. She is the author of the anthology, Love Inspired. *Connect with Nina at www.Dreams-N-Action.com.*

Carol O. Carriere

Drownproofing

Anxiety is love's greatest killer. It makes others feel as you might when a drowning man holds on to you. You want to save him, but you know he will strangle you with his panic.
—Anais Nin

I was the kid who hated summer camp, and I mean ferociously. But being a dutiful child of well-meaning parents, I would obediently go. I literally got nauseous every day. The black and yellow markings on the school bus signified torture. I oozed fear and worry when I saw it arrive in its fake-cheery way with its requisite sun-shiny, sing-songy campers. That excruciating anxiety was due to one activity and one alone: swimming.

I could not seem to figure out how to hold my breath underwater. I would try, and try, and try, trusting the oft-repeated advice about how to do it. And every time, after a few seconds, my lungs would ache and my nasal passages would feel as though miniature knives had been floating in the water and had gushed in and were stabbing me.

I was completely content and marvelously engaged and capable as a dog-paddler. Except, of course, when my active imagination saw the pool drain open, the rush of water down the pipe to goodness knows where, and I would imagine myself being pulled underwater to drown painfully.

Growing up, this swimming handicap continued to plague me. A gregarious preteen, I became a wall weasel whenever it came to water sports. I would hug the sides of the pool and try to be inconspicuous, lest one of my friends notice me and wonder why I wasn't diving for pennies or cannonballing into the deep end. On the rare occasions I would allow myself to be cajoled into jumping off the diving board, I would summon all of my courage, plug my nose with my right hand and plunge to the depths below, praying I would rise to the surface. *Don't drown. Don't drown. Don't drown.*

My close relatives were sailors and part-time fish impersonators and could all water ski. Family vacations were a torture to me. I

That excruciating anxiety was due to one activity and one alone: swimming.

schemed about how I could get out of swimming, or even going near the water. *Maybe I could wish for one long, continuous period and be off the hook.*

After marriage, children, divorce, my restaurant burned to the ground. Without a clear future, I was deeply depressed. I dug deep into my childhood dreams and joined the Naval Reserve. I didn't want the military to own me, I just wanted to be a flight engineer and play with big-kid toys—and render service, service to myself, to my country and to my fellow lost travelers.

Navy boot camp was a terrible experience, full of angst and discomfort. Thankfully, the universe did not challenge me to swim. As long as I could jump from a platform, hold my nose and dog-paddle to the surface with my clothes on, I was fine. *I could do this!*

I joined and began my journey toward becoming a flight engineer in the United States Navy. But the monster in my closet, the nightmare of my liquid worries, would rise up and penetrate the fabric of my psyche yet again.

The monster came disguised as the Swim Physiology ("Swim-Phys") test required to qualify for air crew. I would have to escape from the "dunker," a mock helicopter flipped upside down into a pool. After crashing below twenty feet of water, helmeted and belted into the aircraft, I would have to wait until all movement ceased, and then swim through a prescribed exit—once with my eyes open, and then blindfolded. Upon reaching the surface, I could catch a quick breath before placing my head in the pool in the dead man's floating position. And I would have to do all of this in full flight gear and boots. If I passed, I would be considered "drownproofed." *Yeah, right. That's impossible. Or at least that's impossible for me.*

It became clear that despite my abject fear, despite my doubts, if I wanted to fulfill my childhood dreams I would have to learn

---

*The old fears and thoughts
rushed into my mind.*

---

how to swim—really swim. I had just three months to overturn a lifetime of fear and water underachievement. No more dog-paddle for me.

In order to pass the test, I would have to prove that I could swim without my right hand plugging my nose. I would have to demonstrate authentic executions of the sidestroke, the back-stroke, the Australian crawl and the butterfly. Again, I would have to do all of this in my flight gear, and for many laps, adding up to over a mile in combined distance. And there would be no time to psych myself up or work through a panic attack midway through—the swimming test would be timed. For me, this test was not just an obstacle I had to overcome; this was my Mount Everest. *How would I find the courage to do this?*

It was, I realize now, no matter of coincidence that during this time I came across a book with a curious title: *A Course in Miracles.* Powerful and simple statements sized up the very reason why anything in life is perceived as difficult or dangerous. It was these lines that resonated at my core: "Nothing real can be threatened. Nothing unreal exists. Herein lies the peace of God."

I was deeply moved by reading these lines, but still mostly focused on what I needed to *do* to overcome my fear, still living in a logistical, worried frame of mind. Pushing down my anxiety, I set out to learn how to swim. The first day at the Patuxent River Navy Base Pool, I noticed a woman very adept at her lap exercise, and asked, "Would you teach me how to swim?" Amazingly, she said yes. Soon I was using a paddleboard and practicing putting my face in the water. Then I took more swimming lessons from the Petty Officer running the Swim-Phys program. *I can do it! They're baby steps, but they count.*

"Nothing real can be threatened. Nothing unreal exists. Herein lies the peace of God."

Emboldened by my progress, I decided to just dive into training—literally. I felt a bit insane signing up for SCUBA diving lessons. This was not a baby step! But I knew I had to face my fear of being underwater for an extended time. *It's probably way more difficult than the dunker. If I can pass the SCUBA diving requirements, then by comparison, the dunker and Swim-Phys will be a cakewalk!*

My newfound courage, however small, would be put to the ultimate test when my SCUBA class performed our checkout dive at a Virginia quarry. Twenty-five feet underwater, we were to remove our masks and reposition them back onto our faces, emptying the masks of water by breathing air back into the mask through our nostrils. As soon as I began the maneuver I panicked because, as usual, I was taking in water. The burbling discomfort as I swallowed, the slight gag of water again and again took me back to all of my past failed attempts to swim underwater. I felt the urge to bolt to the surface, but I knew I would surely be disqualified, and that the sudden changes in pressure would wreak havoc on my body.

The old fears and thoughts rushed into my mind, but I kept telling myself, *You have to show them you are NOT a threat to your own safety.* Then, just as I was about to gag on copious sips of water, I heard the words from *A Course in Miracles:* "Nothing real can be threatened. Nothing unreal exists. Herein lies the peace of God."

The words resonated in my plexus and I relaxed. *You are so real, Carol. Drowning is a fantasy, because you are trained to do this. You will not drown.* I choked a bit, but then amazingly, the water intake stopped. I calmed. I stayed at the bottom and successfully cleared my mask! I overcame my fear! I felt so powerful and calm and connected to all life. *Nothing real can be threatened.* It was this cathartic moment of possibly failing the checkout dive's most treacherous maneuver that I learned I could do it. There was truly nothing to fear but fear itself.

When the day arrived to face the dunker, not only was I prepared to face my demons, I actually relished the chance to vanquish them. I passed the Swim-Phys "drownproofing" test with flying colors. I eagerly placed my head in the water, returning to the surface only for quick breaths. While others became exhausted thrashing to stay afloat, I was peaceful and purposeful. The laps were long and physically tiring, but I wasted no energy on anxiety. During the exercise, I was so calm and methodical that the instructor feared for my safety. He sent divers after me, mistaking my serenity for semi-consciousness.

To be freed from fear is a wondrous gift. I look back and realize that what I thought was a given was only a paradigm. I no longer drown in a sea of need. Fear only grows smaller in facing it down; it can only prosper when it is unchallenged and avoided, when we bully ourselves into believing it is real. *Nothing unreal exists. We are real.*

Carol O. Carriere is just your average local "WHICH"-Doctor (inner GPS) and human reckoning aid. She resides in Pensacola, FL with her Navy neurologist husband and assists patient people with learning to trust their baby steps back to finding themselves since they have concluded (erroneously) that they have gotten lost. She is a noted technician in her ability to help clients successfully recalibrate their emotional guidance system. Carol is the co-founder of The Joy Factor Research Initiative, a project aimed at finding empirical evidence linking and identifying the positive correlation of a sense of personal happiness and fearlessness with the most powerful medical prophylactic against all dis-eases existing in the human condition. She is also a restaurateur and game developer. Connect with Carol at www.GuruGarden.net.

Jana Kohl, PsyD

Walking the Walk

If I am not for myself, who will be for me? But if I am only for myself, who am I? If not now, when?
—Hillel, Jewish leader (b.110 B.C.E.)

Ever since I was a kid I cared about justice and stopping abuse of any kind. At age nineteen, I worked for the Simon Wiesenthal Center for Holocaust Studies. In my struggle to understand how the Holocaust occurred, I thought of Einstein's words: "The world is a dangerous place to live; not because of the people who are evil, but because of the people who don't do anything about it." I wanted to be someone who did something.

Years later, a friend asked me to view footage of what goes on behind closed doors in animal-based industries. What I saw onscreen was nothing short of legalized torture. I was curled in a fetal position by the time the footage ended and sobbed for hours. I felt shock, horror, grief, rage and utter helplessness. *This is going on everywhere, all the time, and no one is stopping it! How can this be?*

Once my eyes were opened, I knew my life would never be the same. Although I'd earned a doctorate in psychology and was poised to go into private practice, I changed my plan and became an animal rights activist, for the same reason I'd worked in Holocaust education years earlier: *Some things are so horrific they cannot be ignored.* That footage exposed the ugly truth about the abuse of animals in every industry—food, clothing, circuses, rodeos, research, puppy mills and more. It was the stuff of nightmares, beyond anything I could have imagined, and like the Nazis' atrocities, this barbaric cruelty was also being accepted by supposedly civilized societies. No matter what it took, I had to tell the world.

But no one would listen—not the politicians I knew, not even family or friends. I felt completely and totally alone. My grief for the animals engulfed me. The horrors seemed even more of an outrage because no one was willing to help them.

"I can't watch that footage," people would say. "I'm too sensitive and it will upset me too much."

In frustration and anger I'd reply, "If you can't bear to watch, how can you ask the animals to endure it? We need to see things ourselves to be moved to change." But my words fell on deaf ears.

One politician saw the horrific footage and said coldly, "It's not on my agenda." I was stunned, disgusted; I learned that politicians receive millions in campaign donations from these industries. Their allegiance and silence are bought.

As a psychologist, part of me understood the response of the average person. We don't like to witness or even hear about painful things, and because we're creatures of habit we don't like making changes. Before I saw the footage, I wore fur, ate animal products and bought a puppy from a woman who kept breeding dogs locked in cages, never allowing them to set foot on grass or see the sun. Perhaps my own ignorance should have prepared me to accept the next twelve years of being ignored, dismissed and even ridiculed for trying to alert people to the horrible truth, but it didn't. The impact it had upon me was devastating.

When an important piece of anti-cruelty legislation that I had helped pass was overturned by corrupt politicians, and when one of the most powerful people in the world reneged on his pledge to help end animal cruelty, I fell into a deep depression. I didn't want to see or speak to anyone or even leave the house. Getting out of bed took a Herculean effort and even when I managed to do so I was too despondent to work, answer emails or return calls. To have brought the information to people at the highest level, only to find out they didn't care, was the most painful and disillusioning moment of my life.

Worst of all, I knew: *The animals' suffering will never end.* That realization was so unbearable that I was in a constant state of physical and mental angst. All hope was gone. I swung between depression, rage and panic over not being able to rescue countless

---

I felt completely and totally alone.

---

animals enduring hell on earth. I had horrific nightmares. As UCLA Professor Tammy Bryant observed, those who witness abuse and try to tell others but are met with indifference or rejection suffer doubly, resulting in greater symptoms of PTSD (Post Traumatic Stress Disorder). I feared that I'd never have the strength or will to take up the fight again and that my days as an activist were over.

I found myself in bed one night staring at the TV in a daze, hoping to escape my despair for a few hours. Flipping through the channels, I happened upon an HBO documentary about feminist Gloria Steinem (*Gloria: In Her Own Words*). She was someone I had always admired for her own lifelong mission to end injustice, and I had been fortunate to have interviewed her for a book I'd written. As I watched her story unfold, I was startled to learn things about her that I'd either forgotten or never fully realized. She, too, had endured many obstacles and feelings of despair in her struggle to raise awareness. She, too, had been ignored, dismissed, ridiculed and even attacked by those who felt threatened by her message of equal rights for all.

By the end of the film I was sitting upright again for what felt like the first time in weeks. A memory from our lunch interview made me sit even taller. When she said, "I'm a vegan," I had nearly dropped my fork. Seeing my surprise, she explained that it was a natural extension of her belief that any form of abuse was unacceptable—whether against women, minorities, gays, children, poor people or animals. She talked of the links between livestock farming and the destruction of the environment, world hunger, human disease and even our economic woes. But mostly she saw it as an issue of compassion.

I was about ninety-five percent vegan back then, but after that day something shifted and going from ninety-five to one-hundred percent was suddenly effortless. I have no doubt that Gloria's commitment inspired me in that, and in so many other ways.

Now here she was again, a beacon of compassion and strength, and a kindred spirit reaching out to me by example. I wasn't alone. Even Gloria Steinem had sometimes felt hopeless and didn't want to leave her home; even someone who had inspired great change

---

I had to keep fighting for the animals.

---

in the world had felt like she couldn't get back up after a defeat, setback or personal attack. Even more inspiring, she was one of the few leaders I'd ever met who went beyond championing her own cause—equal rights for women—and spoke up for any who were voiceless and exploited. She has made their plight hers. That's what I call "walking the walk."

I watched the film twice to ensure that her example of perseverance would stay with me, remembering how she kept getting up off the mat, no matter how many times others tried beating her down. I had spent far too many days and nights in self-imposed isolation after suffering setbacks and betrayals; for the first time in a long time I felt ready to get back in the ring. I found my courage again, the voice inside me rising up and gaining strength for the next great push. I had to keep fighting for the animals.

One of the first things I did was accept a request to speak before the Irvine California City Council, which was considering a ban on circuses, rodeos and the sale of animals at pet stores. When the fateful day arrived to step up to the podium, I spoke in a clear, strong voice before the council. "You are my heroes," I began. Unlike so many politicians, who were dismissive of animal cruelty, here was a humane council, led by a compassionate mayor. I was proud of them, and of my reawakened voice.

When the mayor called for a vote, I held my breath. And when he proclaimed the four-to-one vote in favor of the ban, it was moment of sheer joy for me and more important—hope for the animals. My faith in politicians was restored. *Some of them do care.* My faith in myself as an activist was renewed, and my voice reclaimed. *I have to use it for those who cannot speak.*

I pray that when I falter, when corrupt powers-that-be stand in the way of compassion, I will always remember the ones who came before me, who didn't give up. No matter the weight of the tragedy I have witnessed, I must go on if I hope to leave behind a better world. Knowing that I'm not alone is both a comfort and a means toward that end.

With our arms linked in solidarity, none of us are alone in our struggle. Your struggle is mine and mine is yours, because as long as any are oppressed—women, children, poor people, minorities, gays and the most voiceless and abused, animals—then none can truly be free. When we finally decide to take up the mantle of each other's cause, *walking the walk* together, what a glorious world this will be!

Jana Kohl, PsyD is a psychologist, author, speaker, artist and advocate for any who are exploited. Connect with Jana at www.DrJanaKohl.com.

Lisa Nichols

Conclusion

You have a dream and a purpose. You may not see the fulfillment of your dream, your purpose, according to your timeline, but if you persist and lean heavily on your unbreakable, unshakable human spirit, *you will get there.*

So often we get discouraged when we feel the pain of rejection, when we put so much in and get nothing in return. The reality is, whether or not you get the results you hope for today, tomorrow, or ten years from now, as long as you continue to put energy in and develop your dream-building muscles, *you will get there.*

Like the authors in this book who so courageously and selflessly shared their truth with you in these pages, know that you are destined for greatness. Your present tense doesn't negate that. Your current circumstances do not define your existence or alter your destiny *one bit.* You have human spirit backing you up, and you will not be deterred. *You will get there.*

Human spirit wants you to live in your greatness, in your possibility. If your greatness requires one more baby step, or one more giant step, human spirit says, "Yes we can, we can, we always could, and we will always be able to." Human spirit talks to you every day; it speaks to the highest part of you, to the greatness in you. And when you strive to live each day in your highest self, *you will get there.*

Human spirit is not illusive, something you have to seek and find. It is right there inside of you, at this very moment, and it always will be. And it does not favor any one person or group; it belongs to all of us. Our human spirit knows no color, nationality,

You have a dream and a purpose.

religion or economic status, and you don't have to be "special," or "perfect" or "chosen" to access it. All you have to do is let go and let human spirit walk with you to greatness. Because when you draw from the limitless well that is human spirit, there is no doubt in my mind, *you will get there.*

About Lisa Nichols

Lisa Nichols, the "Breakthrough Specialist," has reached millions around the world with her powerful message of empowerment, service, excellence and gratitude. Founder of Motivating the Masses and CEO of Motivating Teen Spirit, LLC, Lisa is a charismatic teacher, speaker and transformational coach. Featured in the self-development phenomenon, *The Secret,* she has appeared on *The Oprah Winfrey Show, Larry King Live* and on NBC's Emmy award-winning reality show, *Starting Over.*

Lisa co-authored *Chicken Soup for the African American Soul, Chicken Soup for the African American Woman's Soul* and *Living Proof: Celebrating the Gifts that Came Wrapped in Sandpaper.* Her book *No Matter What!: 9 Steps to Living the Life You Love* hit six bestseller lists, including *The New York Times,* and has been translated into twenty-five languages. Lisa has been honored with many awards for her empowering work, including the Humanitarian Award from South Africa. Connect with Lisa at www.Lisa-Nichols.com.

We invite you to experience the
Unbreakable Spirit MULTIMEDIA book.

Now that you've read these moving stories, you can also view the online version of UNBREAKABLE SPIRIT on your computer or iPad in an exciting, next-generation multimedia format.

Adding AUDIO and VIDEO conversations to the text, the co-authors share more knowledge and inspiration to help you become the champion of your own life.

We offer you a GIFT of several chapters from the *Unbreakable Spirit* multimedia book at:

www.UnbreakableSpiritBook.com

If you wish to buy the complete multimedia book, please use this coupon code to receive a substantial discount.

Coupon Code — Book8

We also invite you to share your thoughts about our books with our community on our Facebook page at:

www.YinspireMediaFacebook.com

We invite you to read and experience several free chapters of other Yinspire Media multimedia books. If you wish to by the complete multimedia books, we invite you to use the coupon codes to receive a substantial discount. You can purchase the print versions of all these books at Amazon.com.

Get Your Woman On
Embracing Beauty, Grace & The Power of Women
www.GetYourWomanOnBook.com
Coupon Code – Book7

Fight For Your Dreams
The Power of Never Giving Up
www.Fight4YourDreams.com
Coupon Code – Book6

Living Proof
Celebrating the Gifts that Came Wrapped in Sandpaper
www.LivingProofMBook.com
Coupon Code – Book5

How Did You Do That!
Stories of Going for IT
www.HowDidUDoThat.com
Coupon Code – Book2

The Law of Business Attraction
Secrets of Cooperative Success
www.LawOfBusinessAttraction.com
Coupon Code – Book1

Transforming Through 2012
Leading Perspectives on the New Global Paradigm
www.2012MultimediaEbook.com
Coupon Code – Book 4

The Wealth Garden
The New Dynamics of Wealth Creation in a Fast-Changing Global Economy
www.WealthGardenBook.com
Coupon Code – Book 3